W9-APA-484

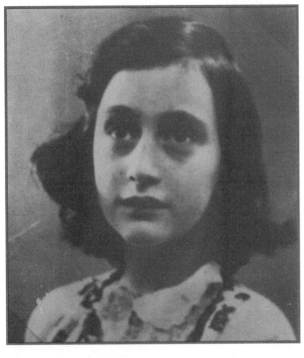

THE HOLOCAUST

Globe Fearon Educational Publisher
A Division of Simon & Schuster
Upper Saddle River, New Jersey

Aaron Breitbart is senior researcher at the Simon Wiesenthal Center in Los Angeles, California. He received his degree in history from Yeshiva University in New York and has devoted most of his career to Holocaust studies and education. In 1986, he was appointed by the California Assembly to a special commission to develop a model curriculum for the study of human rights and genocide. Mr. Breitbart was among those recently portrayed in the television movie, "The Infiltrator" and the book, *In Hitler's Shadow*.

Rose Ann Mulford is a high school social studies teacher in the Livingston, New Jersey Public Schools. She received a Bachelor of Arts degree in elementary education at Trenton State College and a Masters degree in Educational Psychology at Montclair State University. Mrs. Mulford has completed graduate work in Constitutional Law and Government at Rutgers University. In addition to United States History, Mrs. Mulford has taught the Holocaust, American Government, Psychology, and Sociology. Her particular field of interest is the History of Women. Mrs. Mulford wrote the first Women's Studies curriculum for Livingston High School. She is the District Affirmative Action Officer.

Mark Weitzman is the Associate Director of Education and the Director of the Task Force Against Hate for the Simon Wiesenthal Center in Los Angeles, California. He is a graduate of New York University and has studied at the Jewish Theological Seminary of America and Bar-Ilan University in Israel. Mr. Weitzman is a frequent lecturer on the Holocaust, anti-Semitism, and extremism. His many articles have appeared in *The Journal of the National Catholic Educational Association* and *Second Opinion: The Journal of Health, Faith and Ethics*, as well as other publications. Mr. Wietzman is a member of the official Jewish-Catholic Dialogue Group of New York and has served as scholar in residence for a number of tours of Eastern Europe and Germany.

Director of Editorial and Marketing: Nancy Surridge
Project Editors: Karen Bernhaut, Ann Clarkson, Lynn Kloss, Carol Schneider
Marketing Manager: Rhonda Anderson
Production Director: Kurt Scherwatzky
Production Editor: Alan Dalgleish
Electronic Page Production: Foca Company
Editorial Development: WestEd, Ink
Photo Research: Jenifer Hixson
Interior Design: Joan Jacobus
Cover Design: Joan Jacobus

Printed in the United States of America 1 2 3 4 5 6 7 8 9 10 00 99 98 97 96

ISBN 0-835-91826-2

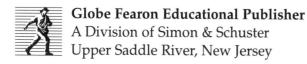

Globe Fearon Educational Publisher
A Division of Simon & Schuster
Upper Saddle River, New Jersey

CONTENTS

Behind the grim brick walls of the concentration camp at Auschwitz, the Nazis pursued their plans for killing the Jews of Europe.

TERMS TO KNOW

- Holocaust
- genocide
- pogrom
- death camp
- ghetto
- concentration camp
- anti-Semitism

THE HOLOCAUST

In the late 1950s, the word *holocaust* became a part of the English language. **Holocaust** comes from a Greek word that means "a sacrifice by burning" or "total burning." The word was added to the English language to describe the systematic murder of six million Jews by Nazi Germany during World War II.

The Holocaust was one of the most devastating events in human history. The Nazis planned to murder all nine million European Jews. Never before had a group of people been singled out for complete extermination simply because of who they were.

The Germans and the Jews were not rivals for territory or power. They had never fought a war with each other. In fact, many Jewish families had lived in Germany for hundreds of years. Many thought of themselves as Germans first and Jews second.

Yet in the 1930s, Germany's Nazi government persecuted the Jews and took away their citizenship. Then during World War II, the Nazis launched a campaign to murder all Jews living in Germany and throughout Europe.

During the Holocaust period, the Nazis also murdered millions of people who were not Jewish. These groups included tens of thousands of people with disabilities, over two million Soviet prisoners of war, and hundreds of thousands of Gypsies. Altogether, the Nazis murdered at least five million non-Jews during World War II.

The Holocaust in History

The Holocaust is not the only example in history of **genocide.** Genocide is the attempt to wipe out an entire people or nation. There have been many acts of genocide in human history. During World War I, the Turks attempted genocide of the Armenians. They murdered nearly one million Armenian people. In the 1970s, the Communist government of Cambodia murdered well over one million of its own people.

The Holocaust is not the only act of mass murder committed against the Jewish people. On their way to conquer the Holy Land, European crusaders massacred thousands of Jews in 1096. Ukrainians rebelling against their Polish rulers murdered over 100,000 Jews between 1648 and 1656. Many Jews died during **pogroms** in Russia during the late 1800s and early 1900s. A pogrom is a violent raid on a Jewish community.

The Unique Tragedy of the Holocaust

The Holocaust *is* different from other acts of genocide for several reasons. It was the only act of genocide attempted by a modern industrial country. Germany was a nation known for its industry, science, and culture. The Nazis used modern methods and technologies to carry out their crimes. They also planned the extermination of the Jews very carefully.

Many scientists, professors, business people, and even doctors took part in the mass murder of Jews. The German government was involved at every level. Thousands of judges, police officers, and government officials helped carry out the Holocaust.

There were important differences between the Holocaust and other acts of murder that the Nazis committed. Among the Nazis' victims, only the Jews were singled out for total destruction. The Nazis considered Russians, Poles, and other groups to be inferior to Germans. However, unlike the Jews, these groups were not targeted for complete extermination. Rather, the Nazis planned to invade and enslave these groups.

The Jews were the only group to be killed simply because of who they were. Driven by their hatred, the Nazis needed no reason to murder Jews. In the eyes of the Nazis, the Jews were completely evil and not fit to live.

Jews were gathered from every country that the German army conquered. The Jews were then brought to **death camps** to be murdered. The Nazis built these death camps specifically to murder Jews. Many other groups of people, such as Gypsies, were murdered in the death camps as well. But the Nazis did not try to find all Gypsies and kill them. They only intentionally hunted the Jews. As a result, two of every three Jews in Nazi-occupied Europe died. No other group of people lost such a high percentage of its people.

The Holocaust is unique in the history of the Jewish people. As you read earlier, the Jews had often suffered from persecution throughout their history. But never before had they faced a systematic attempt to kill every single one of them. Nothing the Jews experienced before had prepared them for the Holocaust.

The Scope of the Holocaust

For many Jews the Holocaust began when they were forced into **ghettos.** A ghetto is a section of a city where a particular group of people is forced to live.

The first Jewish ghettos under the Nazis were set up in 1939. Often the Nazis surrounded the ghettos with brick walls and barbed wire. Movement in and out of the ghettos was strictly controlled. Any Jew caught trying to escape was shot on the spot. The ghettos were crowded and unsanitary. Hundreds of thousands of Jews died of starvation and disease. During the first six months of 1941, over 5,000 people starved to death in the Lodz ghetto. In Case Study 3, you will read about the Warsaw ghetto—the largest of the ghettos.

Some Jews between the ages of 14 and 60 considered fit to work were sent to slave labor camps. Many slave laborers, both Jews and non-Jews, died from the terrible conditions in the camps.

Other Jews were sent to **concentration camps**, where they were starved, beaten, and intentionally worked to death. The Nazis called their system "extermination through labor." The concentration camps claimed the lives of millions of Jewish and non-Jewish people.

The largest numbers of Jews were killed at six death camps. As you have just read, the death camps were highly organized factories designed specifically to carry out the murder of Jews. The largest of these camps was called Auschwitz. You will read more about Auschwitz and the other death camps later in this book.

The Jews who died in the Holocaust came from all over Europe. About 160,000 of them were German Jews. However, one of the largest Jewish communities before World War II was in Poland. About 3.3 million Jews lived there. The Nazis murdered 90 percent of them—about 3 million people. They also murdered 1.5 million Jews from the Soviet Union. Tens of thousands of Jews from France, Belgium, Holland, Yugoslavia, Czechoslovakia, Romania,

Rounded up and marked for death, a group of gypsy prisoners await instructions from their German captors during their first hours in the Belzec concentration camp. Not even children were spared.

Bulgaria, Latvia, Lithuania, Greece, and other countries also died.

Only 300,000 Jews whom the Nazis rounded up survived the war. In addition, over 1.5 million Jews who lived in Europe in 1939 survived. Some of them lived in hiding in Nazi-controlled areas. Others escaped or lived in countries or areas that were not under direct Nazi control.

Hard Times in Germany

How were the Nazis able to come to power in Germany? One reason was World War I. After four bitter years of fighting, Germany was defeated in the war. The victorious Allies led by Great Britain and France blamed Germany for the war. They demanded that Germany pay a huge amount of money for the damage that the war caused. Those payments made it difficult for Germany to financially recover from the war. The defeat in the war also left many Germans looking for someone to blame.

After World War I, the German people overthrew their emperor and set up a democratic government. For the first time in its history, Germany had a democratic government. But Germany's young democracy could not solve the country's economic problems. During the early 1920s, Germany's economy began to fail. In 1923, the economy collapsed. Germany's currency became worthless, and millions of people lost their savings. This first crisis passed, and Germany again recovered. There was hope that the future would be brighter.

The good times did not last, however. In 1929, there was another economic crisis. This one was much worse than anything seen before. In October 1929, the price of stocks in the U.S. stock market collapsed. It was the beginning of

The Nazis increased their appeal to the German people by ceremony, fanfare, and loud and noisy meetings. Here, during a 1934 meeting in Berlin, thousands of German youth give the Nazi salute to a guard of young people.

the Great Depression. It spread from the United States to the world's major industrialized nations, including Germany.

For Germany, it was the third time in a generation that the country had suffered economic disaster. People lost their homes and went hungry. There was no sign that conditions would improve. By 1932, about 40 percent of German workers were unemployed. Now more Germans than ever looked for someone to blame for their troubles. Millions of Germans lost faith in democracy, which seemed unable to solve their problems. As the depression continued, the political parties that opposed democracy gained strength.

The Rise of the Nazis

One political party in Germany said it had a simple answer to Germany's problems. It was the National Socialist German Workers Party, or Nazi party. Its leader was Adolf Hitler, who was a fanatical anti-Semite. **Anti-Semitism** is the hatred of Jews. The mere fact that a person is a Jew is enough reason for an anti-Semite to hate that person. It is based on the belief that all Jews are evil.

The Nazi party told the German people that Germans were the superior race. They called this race the "Aryan" race. All other peoples were inferior. Hitler said the Jews were Germany's greatest enemy and had caused all of its problems. He also said that the Germans must destroy the Jews, or the Jews would destroy them.

Although Germany had a long history of anti-Semitism, the Nazi party did not win many votes during most of the 1920s. This changed suddenly with the Great Depression. Between 1929 and 1930, the number of Nazis elected to the German parliament jumped from 12 to 107. By 1932, the Nazis held 230 seats, more than any other single party. As leader of the Nazi party, Hitler became Chancellor of Germany in 1933. The chancellor is the head of the German government. Within a few months, Hitler used his position to destroy Germany's democratic

system. Germany became a Nazi dictatorship with Hitler as its all-powerful dictator.

Hitler's Nazi government began to persecute the Jews of Germany. The Nazis used terror and violence against the Jews and anyone else who dared to oppose the Nazis' policies.

A fanatical anti-Semite, Adolf Hitler was determined to destroy the Jews. Here, Hitler gives the Nazi salute to his followers.

The Road to World War II

Hitler also expanded Germany's borders by invading its weaker neighbors. In March 1938, he took over Austria. In the fall of that year, he seized part of neighboring Czechoslovakia. On September 1, 1939, Hitler sent the German army into Poland, Germany's eastern neighbor. When that happened, Great Britain and France came to Poland's defense. They were determined to stop German aggression. World War II had begun.

Shortly after the German army entered Poland, the Polish Jews were put in ghettos. They were later sent to labor camps and concentration camps. The terrible conditions in these places quickly killed enormous numbers of people.

In June 1941, Germany invaded the Soviet Union. Special units attached to the German army immediately began murdering hundreds of thousands of Soviet Jews. Within months the Germans began using poison gas to murder Jews. The killing would not stop until Germany's defeat in 1945.

Why Study the Holocaust?

The Holocaust is one of the darkest episodes in human history. It is a very difficult subject to learn about and discuss. Yet it is extremely important to understand the Holocaust.

One reason to study the Holocaust is to be sure that it is remembered. If one of the greatest

As the war ended, the gruesome reality of the Nazi death camps became known to the world. Here, stunned U.S. troops walk among the piles of bodies—all victims of the Nazi horrors.

crimes in history is forgotten, then those who committed the crime will escape judgment.

We must also study the Holocaust to remember its millions of victims. The Holocaust destroyed Jewish communities all over Europe. Many Jews left behind diaries, poems, artwork, and other evidence of their suffering and their struggle to survive and keep their dignity. As we learn about their lives and horrible deaths, we defeat the Nazis' attempt to label the Jews as evil or less than human.

The Holocaust also warns us of the terrible power of anti-Semitism. Anti-Semitism has a long and destructive history and is still with us.

We must also study the Holocaust because it is part of a larger history. The Holocaust is one of a long list of terrible crimes that human beings have committed against each other. The Holocaust therefore warns us that prejudice against any group can lead to disaster. A philosopher and Holocaust survivor named Primo Levi explained:

> *If the world could become convinced that Auschwitz never existed, it would be easier to build a second Auschwitz, and there is no assurance it would devour [finish off] only Jews.*

The Holocaust also is a lesson about how modern skills and technology can be misused. It serves as a warning that there is a dark side to the modern world

Finally, the Holocaust speaks to us about the value of human life. The Sixth Commandment says: "Thou shall not murder." This short message is perhaps the most important lesson of the Holocaust.

Thinking It Over

1. How is the Holocaust different from other acts of genocide?
2. How do Primo Levi's words explain why the study of the Holocaust is important to everyone?

THE JEWISH WORLD BEFORE THE HOLOCAUST: A RICH HERITAGE

The painter Mark Chagall painted scenes that showed traditional Jewish life in Eastern Europe. Here, a man holds the Torah, the Jewish Bible.

CRITICAL QUESTIONS

■ What was Jewish culture in Europe like before the Holocaust?

■ How does persecution affect its victims' lives?

TERMS TO KNOW

■ Diaspora

■ synagogue

■ rabbi

■ assimilate

■ Yiddish

ACTIVE LEARNING

After you read this case study, you will be asked to create a time line of Jewish history based on the information in the case study. As you read, take notes about events and dates mentioned in the case study. Also, look for the Active Learning boxes. They will offer tips to help you complete your notes and time line.

The city of Jerusalem had been transformed by King Solomon into a great capital. Solomon built a temple dedicated to God, which was destroyed by Roman conquerors in 70 A.D. After the Roman conquest, the Jews were exiled from their homeland to distant parts of Europe and Asia.

Heinz Kissinger and Naftali Saleschutz were born only three years apart. Heinz was born in 1923 and Naftali in 1920. Both were Jewish children who lived in Europe. Yet, they grew up in very different worlds.

Heinz was born in a large town in Germany. Naftali was born in a small town in Poland. Both boys were raised in Jewish communities in countries where the majority of the population was Christian.

The Jewish communities of Germany and Poland had some similarities. However, there were also many differences. In this case study, you will learn about these similarities and the differences. You will also read about Jewish life in Europe before the Holocaust.

1 Jewish Life in Europe

Long before the Jews came to Europe, they lived in the Jewish kingdom of Judea. This region is located in what is now the country of Israel in the Middle East. In the early part of the 1st century A.D., the Romans conquered the region. Shortly afterward, Judea began to revolt.

In 70 A.D. a huge Roman army conquered and destroyed Jerusalem, the capital of Judea. The Romans had successfully crushed the Jewish revolt.

The Jewish Diaspora

After defeating the Jews, the Romans murdered and enslaved tens of thousands of them. Many more were exiled, or driven out of the region. Some of the exiled Jews moved east to Central Asia, where Jewish communities already existed. Others moved west into Europe.

Some Jews already lived in Europe, mainly in Greece and Italy. But the Jews who fled westward in 70 A.D. settled in other European lands. They and their families spread the Jewish **Diaspora** to most of Europe. The Diaspora is the scattering of Jews across the world after exile from their ancient homeland. Over the next several hundred years, Jews formed communities in Spain, Germany, France, and other parts of Europe.

Building Communities

Gradually, the Jews of Europe built communities with rich cultural traditions. These Jewish communities centered around **synagogues.** Synagogues are Jewish houses of prayer and religious study. The Jews relied on their Bible, called the Torah, and the Talmud for guidance. The Torah gives Jews their overall moral code. The Talmud is a code of laws and discussions. The Jews used the Talmud to help them solve the problems of everyday life.

The Jews had skills that allowed them to participate in European life. Many Jews were craftsmen and merchants. Others were active in industries such as dyeing, silk weaving, and glassblowing. Many Jews knew several languages. They also had contacts with Jewish communities outside of Europe. Their language skills and outside contacts made them helpful to rulers as diplomats. One such diplomat was Isaac of Aachen.

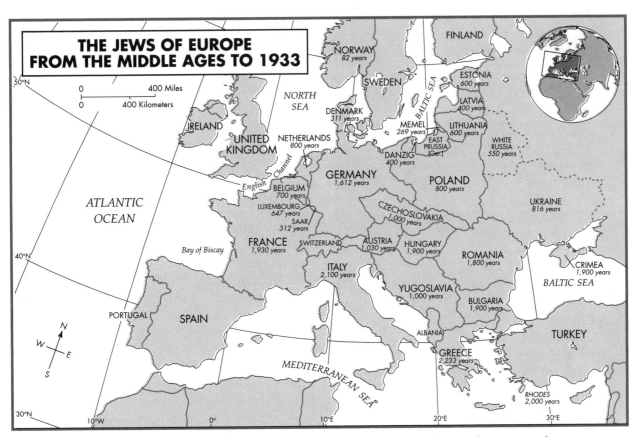

By the 1930s, Jews had lived in most countries of Europe for more than a thousand years. In what country shown on the map had Jews lived the longest by the 1930s? In what countries had they lived for more than 1,500 years?

Isaac of Aachen

When Issac of Aachen set out on his journey, he never imagined that he would be away for four years. The emperor Charlemagne had asked Isaac to make contact with a ruler in the Middle East. Charlemagne was the most important European ruler during the late 700s and early 800s, so of course Isaac agreed.

For a long time, Charlemagne heard nothing about Isaac's mission. Then, in 801, a report to the emperor said that Isaac finally "was on his return journey, laden with great gifts." One of the gifts certainly was great. It was an elephant—the first one ever seen in France!

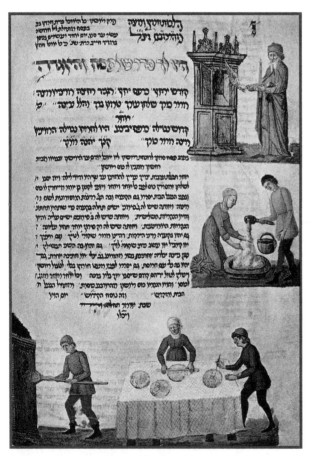

Hebrew books often included pictures of the traditions and customs of the Jewish people. This book illustrates preparations for the Passover holiday. On Passover, Jews commemorate their ancestors' freedom from slavery in ancient Egypt.

The Soncino Family

Jewish communities in Western Europe continued to grow from the 900s to the 1200s. Communities in Germany, France, England, and Spain prospered. Jews moved to Italy and other countries as well. One Jewish family who settled in Italy was the Soncino family.

The Soncino family moved from Germany to Italy during the 1400s. They moved because Jews were being expelled from several German cities at the time. In Italy, the family settled in the small northern town of Soncino. They took the town's name as their family name.

The Soncino family became famous printers of books. The man who began the printing business in Italy was Israel Nathan Soncino, a former physician.

In 1484, the Soncinos published their first Hebrew book. It was the Talmud. Four years later, they printed the first complete Torah. It was a beautiful book that included over 400 drawings.

The Soncino family's business spread to Greece and Turkey. Over the years, the Soncinos produced over 140 Hebrew books, as well as books in Italian and Latin.

Rabbis and Scholars

Jewish religious leaders are called **rabbis.** They are expected to be teachers and set a good example for others. The Jewish communities of the Diaspora could not have survived without the work and sacrifice of the rabbis. When a Jewish community was under attack by Christians, the rabbis were among the first victims.

There were many rabbis, scholars, and teachers among the Jews. One of the greatest of them was Rabbi Gershom ben-Judah (960–1028). He founded an academy for studying the Talmud in Germany. Rabbi Gershom also developed rules that helped Jews manage their daily lives.

Several of the rabbi's rulings were helpful to women. He said that a man could not divorce his wife against her will. Rabbi Gershom also was concerned with a person's right to privacy. He ordered people not to read mail addressed to someone else.

Another outstanding scholar was a rabbi known as Rashi of Troyes (1040–1105). Troyes was a town in France where about 50 Jewish families lived.

Rashi wrote about many subjects. He influenced Jewish communities throughout Europe. One of Rashi's most important works was an explanation of the Torah. His goal was to help ordinary people learn the Torah. He wrote his explanations in clear and simple language that almost everyone could understand. Rashi's work influenced Christian scholars as well as Jews.

Rashi's most important accomplishment was his explanation of the Talmud. It is a work that has great influence even today.

The Jewish community in Spain produced many scholars as well. Jews in Spain became leading doctors, statesmen, poets, philosophers, mathematicians, navigators, astronomers, and businessmen. Judah Halevi (1075–1141) was one of the greatest poets in Jewish history. He also wrote an important book in which he defended the Jewish religion.

Well-educated Spanish Jews often knew several languages. They used that knowledge to serve as translators. Jews translated works from Arabic into European languages. These translations helped bring knowledge of the Arab world to Europe.

Thinking It Over

1. (a) What is the Diaspora?
   (b) Where did Jews go after the Romans sent them out of Judea?
2. Jews have sometimes been called the "people of the book." Based on what you have read, why do you think this might be so?

Active Learning: Be sure to note some of the dates mentioned in this section for your time line of Jewish history. What are some of the most important dates to include? Why?

2 The Problem of Persecution

Even before the Holocaust, the Jews of Europe often faced discrimination and persecution. Conditions varied from country to country and from year to year. At a given time, conditions for Jews might be good in one country and bad in another. The situation often changed within countries. Jews could be living peacefully with their neighbors one year and be victims of brutal violence the next.

"I Hate the Jews"

Why were the Jews singled out to be persecuted? The answer is anti-Semitism. For a long time, anti-Semitic teachings were part of the teachings of Christianity, and Christianity was the religion that most Europeans practiced.

St. John Chrysostom lived in the 300s. He accused the Jews of being less than human. He wrote that "the Jews sacrifice their children to Satan." He also told his followers: "I hate the Jews." His views were repeated by others throughout the centuries.

Because of anti-Semitism, terrible lies about the Jews, like the one St. John Chrysostom told, were spread. The Jews were accused of crimes they could not possibly have committed. One of the worst lies was that the Jews killed Christian children and used their blood in religious services. Jews also were blamed for disasters.

For example, many Christians blamed the Jews for the Black Death, an epidemic that swept Europe in the 1300s.

Because of anti-Semitism, Jews suffered from discrimination even when times were fairly peaceful. By the 800s, Church laws made it almost impossible for Jews to be farmers. Jews therefore had to make their living in other ways. Many of them became merchants.

Despite some discrimination, most European Jews lived fairly peacefully among their Christian neighbors for a long time. As craftsmen, merchants, scholars, and physicians, Jews played an important part in European communities.

Active Learning: The portion of the text below has some important dates that you might want to note for your time line. Find out when Jews were expelled from various countries in Europe.

"Why Do You Act So Cruelly?"

Conditions for Jews changed for the worse in the 11th century. In 1096, the First Crusade began.

Hundreds of years before the Holocaust, the Jews of Europe faced discrimination and persecution. When bad times hit Europe, the troubles were blamed on the Jews. This scene shows a brutal attack on the Jewish population of Frankfurt, Germany in 1614.

The Crusades were a series of Holy Wars that Christians waged to take Jerusalem back from the Turks. As they marched through Germany and other countries, anti-Semitic crusaders murdered thousands of Jews.

In the following centuries, Jews were driven from many countries in Western Europe. Jews were expelled from England in 1290 and from France in 1394. During this period of history, the Jews of Germany were massacred and expelled from many places within Germany.

In several other countries, the story was the same. Where Jews were not expelled, they were forced to live apart from Christians. The sections of cities where Jews were forced to live were called ghettos.

In 1492, Jews who refused to convert to Catholicism were expelled from Spain. These Spanish Jews had ancestors that had lived in Spain for more than 1,000 years. Over 150,000 Spanish Jews suddenly became homeless refugees. As the Jews prepared to leave Spain, one of their leaders sent a note to the king. He asked simply, "Oh Majesty, save your loyal subjects. Why do you act so cruelly toward us?" The king did not respond.

Many of the Jews who were forced to leave Western Europe moved to Eastern Europe. In the mid-1300s, many Jews settled in Poland. Although there was anti-Semitism in Poland, Jews lived fairly peacefully there for the next 300 years. In the mid-1600s, Poland weakened and disorder began. When that happened, the Jews were the first to suffer.

Thinking It Over

1. For what kinds of acts were Jews blamed by Christians?
2. When were Jews who refused to convert to Catholicism expelled from Spain?

3 The Two Worlds of Naftali and Heinz

As you have read, Jews had established communities in both Germany and Poland. By the time the Holocaust occurred, these communities were hundreds of years old. The events of the Holocaust deeply affected the Jews of both Germany and Poland. As you will see, it changed forever the lives of Heinz Kissinger and Naftali Saleschutz.

The World of Heinz Kissinger

By the time Heinz was born, his family had been living in Germany for at least 200 years. During that time, the Kissingers led a life fairly typical of German Jews. The Kissingers practiced the Jewish religion. Heinz, like many Jewish children, received a thorough Jewish education.

At the same time that they preserved their Jewish traditions, the Kissingers **assimilated** to German culture. To assimilate is to become more like the majority culture.

The Kissingers and other Jewish families spoke German and sent their children to German schools. They dressed like Germans and admired German culture. On the whole, they behaved like most other German families. In fact, the Jews of Germany were the most assimilated of all European Jews.

Heinz's father, Louis, was a teacher. He taught in a school run by the government where German children of all religions studied. He read widely and loved German and other European literature.

Even the name Kissinger was German. Heinz's great-great-grandfather, Meyer, made it the family name in 1817. However, Meyer and his sons and grandsons all had typical Jewish first names. When Heinz and his brother Walter were born, their parents gave them typical German first names to go with their German last name.

The World of Naftali Saleschutz

About half the people in the small Polish town where Naftali Saleschutz was born were Jewish. The rest were Catholic, the faith of the Polish majority. Naftali's family had lived for generations in the country where he was born.

Unlike the Kissingers, the Saleschutz family and most Polish Jews lived a traditional Jewish life. They strictly followed the customs and laws of the Jewish religion. Naftali is a Jewish name taken from the Bible.

At home the Saleschutz family spoke **Yiddish.** Yiddish is a language that was developed by European Jews between the 800s and the 1100s. It is a mixture of German, Hebrew, and the languages of Eastern Europe, such as Polish.

Although some Polish Jews had assimilated to Polish culture, most did not. Their clothing, appearance, religious practices, and language marked most Polish Jews as different from their Christian neighbors. Years later as an adult, Naftali recalled that he had dressed "in a long black coat and with a traditional cap, wearing earlocks." Earlocks are long uncut sideburns. Many religious Jewish men and boys still wear earlocks today.

As you can see, the lives of Heinz and Naftali were quite different, since German Jews and Polish Jews differed in many ways. Yet, each community added to the rich culture of the European Jews.

The Jews of Poland

Despite murderous attacks by anti-Semites, the Polish Jewish community became one of the largest in Europe. By the early 1900s, the Jews in Poland numbered over three million.

Many Polish Jews lived in small towns and villages. They spoke Yiddish and practiced traditional Jewish customs. They worked as shopkeepers, tailors, and carpenters.

As time went on, the Polish Jewish community began to change. Many Jews had

A Good Book to Read

Image Before My Eyes: A Photographic History of Jewish Life in Poland, 1864–1939, edited by Lucjan Dobroszycki and Barbara Kirshenblatt-Gimblett, Schocken Books, New York, 1977.

This book uses over 340 photographs to tell the history of a large and creative community. The pictures show you both the best and the worst of times. *Image Before My Eyes* lets you visit a people and a world that the Nazis destroyed.

moved to Poland's cities. Over 25 percent of all Polish Jews lived in Poland's five largest cities.

Many of the Jews that lived in large cities had assimilated to Polish culture. Although many spoke Yiddish, they also spoke Polish and sent their children to Polish schools. They dressed and looked like the Christian Poles whom they lived and worked with in the cities.

Whether they lived in villages or cities, all Polish Jews faced the reality of anti-Semitism. After World War I ended, there were deadly riots against Polish Jews. In the 1930s, the Polish government passed laws that discriminated against Jews. Worst of all, right next door in Germany the Nazis were coming into power.

The Jews in Modern Germany

In the early 1900s, the Jewish community of Germany was the most successful in Europe. About 560,000 Jews lived in Germany in 1925. Although they made up less than one percent of the population, they played a large role in German life.

German Jews were among Germany's leading writers, artists, scientists, and doctors.

GOING TO THE SOURCE

Religion in the Life of Jews in Polish Villages

Naftali Saleschutz grew up in the village of Kolbuszowa in Poland. In the 1920s and 1930s, religion was an important part of the life of Jews who lived in this type of village. Below is Naftali's description of the life he knew as a boy.

There were about 2,000 Jews in Kolbuszowa, about 95 percent of whom were observant, pious people.... Before a Jew went to sleep at night he had to put a glass of water near his bed. This was because the first thing he was to do on awakening in the morning was to [clean] himself, wash his fingertips, then say a prayer of thanks to God for having restored [brought] him to life after sleep. From this simple practice there is much to be learned. Never was God far from the thoughts of any Jews, or from our lips. Few sentences passed without a "thank God.." From the morning on and throughout the working day the Jew was mindful of his religious [duties], woven as they were into the fabric of everyday life. Never could we become so [involved] in the world as to forget ... whose children we were ... [and] to whom we owed thanks. Rather we would pause, say our blessing or prayer, and only then resume [continue] whatever activity we were about [to do].

Eating food always brought forth prayers. One said a prayer before drinking water, but the responsibility did not end there. Later on, drinking another glass of water brought you to a repetition [repeat] of the prayer. Prayers before putting on new clothes, prayers before going to sleep—such occasions for prayer are not surprising. But in the course of a given day prayers must also be given in response to lightening or thunder, or even on sighting a rainbow. The prayers were a common vocabulary taught to us as children; they were as natural to us as anything we did.

From Norman Salsitz, *A Jewish Boyhood in Poland: Remembering Kolbuszowa.* New York: Syracuse University Press, 1992, pp. 140–141.

1. Why did a Jew in Kolbuszowa put a glass of water near his bed when he went to sleep?
2. Give one example of how religion affected the everyday lives of the Jews of Kolbuszowa.

The scientist Albert Einstein (1879–1955) was a famous German Jew.

Walter Rathenau (1867–1922) was a successful and well-respected businessman and statesman. During World War I, he had run Germany's economy. After Germany lost the war, he played a leading role in helping Germany recover from its defeat. In 1922, he was murdered by an anti-Semitic extremist. Rathenau's death was a symbol of the dangers facing German Jews.

While they contributed to German culture, German Jews did not neglect their Jewish traditions. They wrote poems and books in Hebrew. The community maintained many Jewish schools and founded many charities for people in need.

"I Am A German, And I Am A Jew."

World War I ended in 1918. From that time until 1932, Germany was a democratic country. For the first time in their history, German Jews enjoyed full equal rights with other Germans. The period from 1918 to 1932 is often called the "finest hour" of German Jewry.

In 1933, a writer named Jakob Wasserman (1873–1933) wrote, "I am a German and a Jew, one as much as the other, the one inseparable from the other." Most German Jews shared Wasserman's attitude.

Unfortunately, the German population as a whole did not share Wasserman's attitude. Many Germans still were influenced by anti-Semitism. They never accepted their Jewish neighbors as complete Germans. They kept what some people called a "glass wall" between themselves and their Jewish neighbors.

In this way, German attitudes toward Jews were similar to Polish attitudes. In both Germany and Poland, the Jews were kept apart from the rest of the country by anti-Semitic prejudice. Without that prejudice, the Holocaust would not have taken place.

The Fates of Heinz and Naftali

When the Nazis came to power in Germany in 1933, many Jews realized that they had no future there. In 1938, Louis Kissinger took his family to the United States. There young Heinz became "Henry." Henry Kissinger grew up to become U.S. Secretary of State and a Nobel Peace Prize winner. His many aunts, uncles, and cousins who remained in Germany died in the Holocaust.

Naftali Saleschutz was still in Poland when Nazi Germany invaded his country in September 1939. In 1942, the Nazis murdered Naftali's entire family. Only Naftali and his brother survived. They were kept alive to work in a labor camp.

Naftali and his brother escaped from the camp and joined a band of Jews that fought the Nazis in the forests. Of the 125 members of the band, only six survived the war. Naftali and his brother were among the six survivors.

In 1947, Naftali and his new wife Amalie came to the United States. Amalie also was a Holocaust survivor. Naftali changed his name to Norman Salsitz. The couple had a daughter and built a new life together.

Just before Naftali's mother was murdered by the Nazis, she sent him a letter. She told him, "Stay alive, and when the war is over let the world know what the Germans did, what murderers they are." Naftali did as his mother instructed. He wrote a book about his life in Poland. It is dedicated "to the Jews from Kolbuszowa who were murdered in the Holocaust."

Thinking It Over

1. What is one similarity between the lives of Heinz and Naftali? What is one difference?
2. Why do you think Polish Jews who moved to the cities were more likely to become assimilated than those who lived in villages?

Case Study Review

Identifying Main Ideas

1. What roles did Jews play in the different countries in which they settled?
2. How did anti-Semitism affect the lives of Jews in Europe?
3. How had the Polish Jewish community changed by the early 1900s?

Working Together

Form a small group. Create a poster or a bulletin board display of Jewish life in Europe before the Holocaust. Your display may include written work, maps, drawn pictures, or copies of pictures from books or magazines. Use your school or local library for additional resources.

Active Learning

Creating a Time Line Review the notes that you took as you read this case study. Create a time line of Jewish history based on your notes. Then illustrate your time line with pictures that you have drawn or cut from magazines and newspapers.

Lessons for Today

As you have read, the Jewish people were forced to leave their homeland of Judea and start new lives in Europe. Have you or any of your friends ever had to move into a new neighborhood, city, or country? What difficulties did you or your friends encounter? Were any of these difficulties similar to those experienced by the Jews? Write a paragraph describing the similarities and the differences.

What Might You Have Done?

Imagine that you are one of a group of Jews who are being expelled from Jerusalem after the Roman conquest in 70 A.D. Together with three or four classmates, decide where you will go. Will you go east or west? To what country will you go? Use an atlas, a classroom map, or a globe to trace the route that you will take to get to your destination. Finally, give reasons for the location you choose.

CRITICAL THINKING

Analyzing Words Used to Attack the Jews

The Language of Thinking

A weighted word is one that may produce emotions of anger, sadness, or guilt in the reader. A weighted word has to be used in a special context, or setting, to be effective. For example, the word "surprise" has no special emotional weight if it is used in the sentence, "We're giving Eileen a surprise party." However, if we use the word in the following context—"a surprise attack on a sleepy town"—it has a great emotional effect.

Writers and speakers try to win you over to their point of view in a number of different ways. One way is by the facts they choose to present or the facts they choose to ignore. Another is the way in which they use words and phrases.

Clear thinkers and writers use facts and specific examples to prove their arguments. Sometimes, however, a writer will include few or no facts to try to persuade you. Instead of using facts and examples, the writer will use weighted words—words that produce good or bad feelings in the minds of the reader. This kind of writing focuses on the reader's emotional response to the argument.

Read the excerpt below. It is from the writings of St. John Chrysostom, whom you read about in this case study. Think about the way in which he has used emotions and made up or ignored facts to shape his argument.

The Jews . . . are worse than wild beasts. . . . The synagogue is a den of scoundrels, the temple of demons [devils] . . . a criminal assembly of Jews, a place of meeting for the assassins [killers] of Christ. . . . The synagogue is a curse. . . . [The Jews] know only one thing: to satisfy their stomachs, to get drunk, to kill and beat each other up. . . . I hate the Jews. . . . I hate the synagogue. . . . It is the duty of all Christians to hate the Jews.

1. In making his argument, the writer has used a number of highly emotional, or weighted, words. List them.

2. Give a definition for each weighted word. Give a word that means just the opposite.

3. Think about what you have learned from this case study about how Jews lived and worshipped. Compare what you know with what the writer has said about Jews. For example, review what you read about Rabbi Gershom ben-Judah. How do his teachings compare with what St. John Chrysostom says about the Jews?

KRISTALLNACHT: THE BEGINNING OF THE END

By 1933, German Jews faced brutal treatment by the Nazis. Here, a Nazi storm trooper stands guard outside a Berlin store. A Jewish star has been painted on a display window. The sign warns all "Germans" not to buy at a store owned by Jews.

CRITICAL QUESTIONS

■ Why do people sometimes try to blame their problems on others?

■ Why do you think most people tend to "follow the crowd?"

TERMS TO KNOW

■ Kristallnacht

■ scapegoat

■ boycott

■ propaganda

■ Gestapo

■ SS

ACTIVE LEARNING

After you have finished reading this case study you will be asked to conduct an interview. Your interview will explore the persecution of Jews before and during Kristallnacht. As you read the case study, take notes about how Kristallnacht affected the lives of Jews. Think about the types of questions you would want to ask someone who experienced or witnessed this event.

In 1938, Leipzig was one of the most beautiful cities in Germany. It was a cultural center and one of the nicest places to live. Many of Germany's outstanding artists had spent time there. Among them were Goethe, Germany's greatest poet, and the famous composer Johann Sebastian Bach.

Fine old houses lined the well-kept streets of Leipzig. In the middle of town stood a huge monument nearly 300 feet high. It was built to commemorate the Battle of Leipzig in 1813. In that battle, armies from Germany and other countries defeated the French emperor Napoleon.

In the early morning hours of November 10, 1938, Leipzig was no longer a beautiful, well-kept city. Angry mobs turned it into a place of violence, destruction, and terror.

Wim van Leer, a visitor from Holland, happened to be walking down the street on the morning of November 10. A truck suddenly drove up to the curb a few houses from where he stood. About 20 young men jumped out of the truck. They were Nazi storm troopers. Storm troopers were soldiers in the Nazi party militia. They regularly attacked Jews and anyone who dared challenge the Nazi government.

Van Leer watched as the storm troopers began their assault, smashing windows and breaking into Jewish homes. He recalled:

Suddenly the third-floor balcony doors were flung open and storm troopers appeared, shouting to their pals below. . . . Next they wheeled an upright piano over the edge. It nosedived into the street below with a sickening crash as the wooden casing broke away.

Enthusiastic mobs soon joined the storm troopers in their destructive work. They smashed the property of Jews, throwing furniture into the street. The mobs smashed store windows and looted the stores. They firebombed Leipzig's synagogues and destroyed the religious objects inside. They viciously beat up any Jews they saw, including women and children. One boy was thrown from a three-story window. Both of his legs were broken in the fall.

These terrible actions were not limited to Leipzig. Similar attacks on Jews and their property took place all over Germany and Austria on the night of November 9 and the morning of November 10.

The destruction that occurred on November 9 and 10 is known as **Kristallnacht**. In English, Kristallnacht means "Crystal Night," or the "night of the broken glass." The Nazis proudly chose that name to describe this period of terror because of the enormous amount of shattered glass that littered the streets after the riots ended. The glass came from damaged and destroyed Jewish homes, stores, and synagogues.

Kristallnacht was planned and carried out by the Nazi party. Adolf Hitler and the Nazis had been in power in Germany since 1933. One of their goals in 1938 was to terrorize Germany's Jews and drive them from the country. Hitler also wanted to use the violence as a way to stir up German anger toward Jews.

Kristallnacht showed that the Nazis were prepared to use extreme violence against the Jews. It signaled the beginning of the end for the Jews of Germany and in other European countries that the Nazis would soon control.

1 Adolf Hitler's Rise to Power

The man who did more than anyone else to bring about the Holocaust was Adolf Hitler. The Nazi party could not have come to power without his leadership. Although the Nazi party had always been prejudiced against Jews, Hitler's burning hatred of Jews became the core of the Nazi party. It made the party even more anti-Semitic and extreme than it had been.

Hitler, however, did not act alone. The Holocaust could not have happened without the active participation of hundreds of thousands of people throughout Europe. It could not have happened without the willingness of millions of people to look the other way as Jews were brutally persecuted.

Hitler's Early Years

Hitler was born in Austria in 1889. Austria is a small German-speaking country on Germany's southeast border. At the time of Hitler's birth, Austria was the center of the Austro-Hungarian empire. The empire split apart into several countries after World War I.

Hitler's mother came from a small village. His father was a minor government official. Shortly after his father died, Hitler dropped out of high school. He went to Vienna, the capital of the empire, with hopes of becoming an artist. He was unsuccessful and remained unemployed in Vienna for several years.

During World War I, Hitler tried to avoid being drafted. However, he eventually joined the German army. Germany and Austria were allies during the war. Hitler was a good soldier and received several medals. He was shocked when Germany lost the war. Like many Germans, he needed someone to blame for the defeat. He blamed the Jews.

After the war, Hitler moved to southern Germany. Once again he was unemployed. He joined the Nazi party and quickly became its leader. After a failed attempt to seize control of the German government in 1923, Hitler spent a short time in prison. There he wrote *Mein Kampf* (*My Struggle*), the story of his life.

A Good Book to Read

The Rise and Fall of Adolf Hitler, William Shirer, Random House, New York, 1984.

Author William Shirer was in Germany during the 1930s. He witnessed the Nazi rise to power firsthand. *The Rise and Fall of Adolf Hitler* tells the story of this sinister leader from his boyhood to his death.

It described his political views and revealed his strong anti-Semitic feelings.

Hitler's Anti-Semitism

Hitler already was a vicious anti-Semite as a young man. He was influenced by the anti-Semitism that was common in both Austria and Germany. Hitler adopted a new version of anti-Semitism that had developed during the last part of the 1800s. Earlier anti-Semitism was based on religion. If a Jew converted to Christianity, he or she would escape persecution.

The new version of anti-Semitism drew its ideas about Jews from a racial perspective. This meant that Jews were considered an evil race. They could not change even if they became Christian. The fact that they had been born Jewish made them evil. Jews would always be a danger to Germany. Therefore, they either had to be driven away or completely destroyed.

These anti-Semitic ideas fit in with Hitler's other theories about race. He believed that the Germans were the superior "Aryan" race. Hitler combined racial and religious anti-Semitism. According to Hitler:

> *Two worlds face one another—the men of God and the men of Satan! The Jew is the anti-man, the creature of another God. He must have come from another root of the human race. I set the Aryan and the Jew over and against each other.*

Hitler made his views about the Jewish race part of the official Nazi program. Hatred of Jews became the focus of that program. Of its 25 points, 8 were about Jews. Point 4 of the Nazi program stated that no Jew could be a German citizen. The argument was based on Hitler's racist ideas about German "blood."

> *Only a member of the race can be a citizen. A member of the race can only be one who is of German blood. Consequently, no Jew can be a member of the race.*

Hitler also believed that Jews had a plan to take over the world. As proof, he cited a book

Combining a message of vicious hatred with a strong personality, Adolf Hitler rose to power in Germany within a few years. He preached his violent message to his followers at crowded demonstrations. Here, right arm outstretched in the Nazi salute, he greets followers shortly after he came to power.

called *The Protocols of the Learned Elders of Zion*. The book was a forgery, or fake. It had been published by the secret police of Russia before World War I. Hitler read it when it was translated into German after the war.

As you read earlier, Hitler felt bitter about Germany's defeat in World War I. Germany also suffered from a deep economic depression. (See the Overview.) Hitler blamed these troubles on the Jews. He and the Nazi party made the Jews into **scapegoats**. A scapegoat is a person who is blamed for the mistakes or crimes of others. In 1923, Hitler told an audience,

> *Do we wish to restore Germany to freedom and power? If yes, then the first thing to do is to rescue it from the Jew who is ruining our country.*

Active Learning: While reading this next section, notice how Hitler convinced the German people to believe in the Nazi's cause. Include these methods in your interview.

Winning Over the German People

How was Hitler able to win over millions of Germans to the Nazi cause? His success began with the desperate situation of the German people after 1929. In that year, a worldwide economic depression began. The depression ruined millions of Germans. They had already suffered financially during World War I and in the early 1920s. Once again their businesses went bankrupt, or they were fired from their jobs. They stopped believing in democracy. Many Germans were ready to listen to the messages on the Nazi posters that said, "Hitler, Our Last Hope."

Hitler's great skill as a speaker helped captivate the German people. He stirred the emotions of tens of thousands of people at huge rallies. He was one of the first politicians who used the radio to reach an audience of millions. Hitler knew how to appeal to German national feeling and mix that appeal with attacks on Jews.

Hitler used anti-Semitism to tell different groups of Germans what they wanted to hear. He told the nation that the Jews were responsible for Germany's defeat in World War I. He told the businesspeople that Jews favored communism.

He told German workers that the Jews were the businesspeople who were taking advantage of them. Through his passionate speeches, Hitler persuaded the German people to blame their problems on the Jews.

Hitler used violence against those people who spoke out against him. He sent Nazi storm troopers into the streets to beat up his opponents. These actions helped Hitler and the Nazis win control of the German government in January 1933. Once they had power, they used it with brutal efficiency.

Thinking It Over

1. How was racial anti-Semitism different from religious anti-Semitism?
2. (a) What is a scapegoat? (b) Why do you think the German people were looking for scapegoats in the 1920s and 1930s?

2 The Nazi Dictatorship and the Jews

Hitler became Chancellor of Germany by legal means. He rose to power according to the rules of Germany's democratic system. However, his first goal when he became chancellor was to destroy democracy in Germany.

He succeeded in a matter of months. In February, the German parliament building burned down. The Nazis blamed the fire on another political party. The Nazis then instituted emergency acts to end freedom of speech and other liberties.

In March 1933, the Nazi government passed a new law that gave Hitler total power for four years. At the same time, the government set up its first concentration camp. It was called Dachau.

Hitler used his power to completely end Germany's democracy. Germany's people had failed to defend their democracy against the Nazis. As a result, the German people soon lived under a dictatorship.

The Nazis attempted to crush all opposition no matter where it came from. These factory workers who protested Nazi policies were lined up, arrested, and shipped off to concentration camps.

"Don't Buy From Jews."

Germany's Jews began to suffer immediately. In March, Nazi storm troopers attacked Jews on the streets of Berlin, Germany's capital. Gangs of 5 to 30 often attacked a single person.

An English journalist saw several attacks. He wrote that people were beaten "until blood streamed down their heads and faces, and their backs and shoulders were bruised. Many fainted and were left lying on the street."

In April, the Nazi government announced that Germans should **boycott** Jewish businesses for one day. To boycott is to refuse to do business or associate with a certain individual or group. Storm troopers stood in front of Jewish-owned stores with signs saying "German people, defend yourselves. Don't buy from Jews." They painted anti-Jewish slogans or the word "Jew" on shop windows. Germans who dared to shop in Jewish stores were insulted and often beaten.

The Violence Continues

After the boycott, violence against the Jews continued. The violent acts of the Nazi storm troopers frightened Germans and Jews alike. It also helped to push Jews out of German society. The violence stirred up anti-Semitism and hostility toward Jews. Many Jews were murdered or arrested on German streets.

The Nazi regime had already built its first concentration camp, called Dachau. The Nazis murdered four Jews in a two-week period at the Dachau concentration camp.

In May, the Nazis burned thousands of books at a huge bonfire in front of the Berlin Opera House. Some of the burned books were by Jewish writers. Others were written by non-Jews who were opposed to the Nazis. The book-burning clearly was more than an attack on Jews. It was a warning to anyone who opposed the Nazis.

At a huge bonfire in front of the Berlin Opera House in 1933, Nazi students unload "un-German" books for the bonfire. Many of the books were classics that had been written by Jewish writers. The sign they wave says "German students march against the un-German spirit."

During 1933, quotas were set up that greatly limited the number of Jews who could attend public schools. Thousands of Jewish children had to leave their schools. They attended private schools that the Jewish community quickly set up.

The Jewish children who remained in the public schools found themselves under constant attack. Frederic Zeller was a nine-year-old student in Berlin in 1933. He remembers how school turned into a nightmare.

Quite a few teachers were now baiting us.... *Ridiculing us in front of the class.*

"Zeller?," questioned my teacher snidely, "that can't be your real name, can it? I bet it was something more like Schmu-le-witz, Or I-Saak-sohn ...right?" [Schmulewitz and Isaacsohn are Jewish-sounding names.]

Then he snapped furiously: "Stand to attention when I'm talking to you. What do you think this is—a Jew school?"

Active Learning: Make notes on how Nazi persecution affected Jewish children like Frederic Zeller. If you could interview Zeller, what questions would you ask him?

The Nuremberg Laws

By the end of 1933, there were signs on thousands of roads, shops, and other places with the message "Jews not wanted." During 1934, a campaign took shape to create "Jew free" villages. Mobs of Nazi supporters entered villages and dragged Jews from their homes. They whipped, beat, and insulted their victims. Some were cruelly murdered.

Thousands of Jews lost their jobs. A decree said that Jews could not inherit farms. Jews found it impossible to keep their businesses alive because of the boycotts and violence.

Frederic Zeller remembered what happened to his parents' store in 1935.

Earlier that spring, another bunch of thugs had started to boycott our store. And this time not just for days at a time. They kept coming back for weeks, blocking our door and molesting people who tried to enter. Very few dared. Our business, already feeble, collapsed.

In the spring of 1934, all "non-Aryans" were banned from serving in the military. By then there were laws forbidding Jews to do most of the things people often take for granted. For example, Jews could not go to public parks, use public swimming pools, or even own a dog.

In September 1935, the Nazi party held a meeting in the town of Nuremberg. They announced two new laws. The first law said that only a person of "German or related blood"

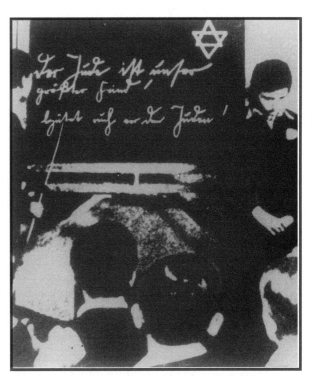

Jewish students are humiliated in front of their classmates. The boys are forced to stand next to a chalkboard on which an anti-Semitic slogan has been written, while another student reads the words aloud: "The Jew is our greatest enemy!"

could be a German citizen. This law stripped the Jews of their German citizenship.

The second law was called the "Law for Protection of German Blood and German Honor." It made marriage between Jews and other Germans illegal. Severe punishment awaited anyone who dared to violate the law.

The Nuremberg laws took away all of the civil rights of Germany's Jews. The laws also completely segregated them from the rest of German society.

There was little the Jews of Germany could do to defend themselves. However, they did what they could to keep their spirits strong. Dr. Leo Baeck was a rabbi in Berlin and the leader of the German Jewish community. He composed a prayer for Yom Kippur (the Day of Atonement) services in 1935. It said in part, "We stand by our faith and our fate. . . . We stand before God. . . . Before him we bow, but we stand upright before men." The Nazis sent Dr. Baeck to prison.

Thinking It Over

1. How did Hitler destroy democracy in Germany?
2. How did the Nuremberg laws push Jews out of German society?

---

3 Nazi Propaganda and Terror

As the campaign against the Jews mounted, millions of German people joined in. They loved Hitler and were prepared to do whatever he said. Frederic Zeller remembered how by 1935, "Jew baiting had become a popular movement." A store across the street from his home put up a sign saying "The Jews are our misfortune." A mob of teenagers beat up religious Jews and set their beards on fire.

"A Big Lie"

Why did people join "the pack?" One reason is that the Nazis were masters of **propaganda.** Propaganda is the spreading of false information to purposely mislead people.

The mastermind of the Nazi propaganda machine was Joseph Goebbels. He controlled and used films, books, radio, newspapers, and even the German educational system to promote the Nazi cause. One Nazi official summed up the main goal of German schools after 1933 when he said, "The whole function of education is to create Nazis." After school, millions of German children went off to the Nazi party's youth organization, called the Hitler Youth.

Goebbels helped turn Hitler into a godlike figure in the eyes of the German people. Goebbels also convinced the people to hate Jews as much as they loved Hitler. No lie was too big for Goebbels. As Hitler himself put it, "The broad mass of a nation will more easily fall victim to a big lie than to a small one." Through the use of propaganda, the Nazis told big lies about the Jews and convinced the German people to believe them.

The Gestapo and the SS

The Nazis had several instruments of terror that they used to enforce their power. The most important of them were the **Gestapo** and the **SS.**

The Gestapo was a police force that the Nazis set up in early 1933. However, the Gestapo was not an ordinary police force. Its mission was not to protect German citizens. Its job was to eliminate all opposition to Hitler and the Nazis. The Gestapo used brutal methods when it arrested and questioned people. Between 1933 and 1945, the Gestapo committed murder and participated in every crime of the Nazi government.

The Gestapo was part of a larger and even more deadly organization called the SS. The SS began in the 1920s as a few men who served as a special guard for Hitler. After 1933, it became the most active instrument of Nazi terror. By 1939, the SS had over 250,000 men.

The SS was headed by Heinrich Himmler. Himmler and the SS spread terror throughout Nazi-controlled Europe. By the early 1940s, much of Europe was under its heel.

The SS controlled Germany's police and had its own military units. It was the SS that took charge of the extermination of Jews. It rounded up Jews and controlled the death camps where they were murdered. The SS was the most efficient killing machine in history.

Thinking It Over

1. What role did Joseph Goebbels play in the Nazi government?
2. What role did the Gestapo and SS play in Nazi Germany?

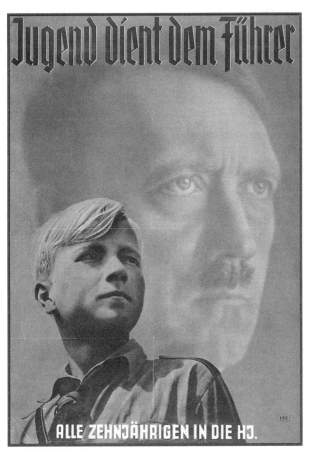

This Nazi propaganda poster is aimed at recruiting young people to the Nazi party. The poster urges "Join the Fuhrer [Leader]." The Nazis perfected the use of propaganda techniques to attack their enemies.

4 The Night of the Broken Glass

Since the Nazis came to power in 1933, they persecuted Germany's Jews. In less than six years, Jews in Germany lost all of their rights. Hundreds of Jews were being murdered on Germany's streets or in concentration camps.

By November 1938, about 30 percent of Germany's Jews had emigrated. Then on November 9, came Kristallnacht. As the Nazi mobs shattered the glass in Jewish homes and stores, they also shattered the last bit of hope that Jews had for a future in Germany.

Utter Destruction

The most common targets of the mobs were Jewish synagogues and the religious objects inside. Every synagogue has at least one copy of the Torah in the form of two large scrolls. It is kept in a wooden closet called an ark. The mobs took special pleasure in destroying these Holy Scriptures.

A Jewish man who witnessed Kristallnacht described a typical scene that occurred in a village in western Germany.

> After a while, the storm troopers were joined by people who were not in uniform; and

suddenly, with one loud cry of "Down with the Jews," the gathering produced axes and heavy sledgehammers. They advanced toward the little synagogue.

The crowd tore the Holy Ark wide open; and the three men who had smashed the Ark threw the Scrolls of the Law of Moses out. They threw them ...to the screaming and shouting mass of people which had filled the synagogue.

Naked and open, the Scrolls lay in the muddy autumn lane; children stepped on them and tore pieces from the fine parchment on which the Law was written.

The Results of Kristallnacht

The results of Kristallnacht were disastrous for Germany's Jews. Ninety-one were killed and thousands more were beaten and tortured. In just one day, the Nazis destroyed over 7,000 Jewish-owned shops and businesses. The mobs burned over 300 synagogues to the ground.

During and immediately after Kristallnacht, the Nazis arrested over 30,000 Jews. They sent them to Dachau and two other concentration camps. Finally, the German government fined the Jewish community one billion marks. The government declared that the Jews were responsible for the riots and should pay for the cleanup costs.

After Kristallnacht about 150,000 Jews fled Germany. However, those who settled in neighboring countries in Europe did not go far enough. In September 1939, Nazi Germany's invasion of Poland marked the beginning of World War II. Suddenly, over three million Polish Jews were in the same terrible situation as Germany's Jews.

Jews had lived for hundreds of years in France, Belgium, Holland, Czechoslovakia, and other countries in Europe. They considered these countries their homelands. But when

The morning after Kristallnacht, Jewish owners of stores sweep the broken glass from the streets.

the Germans invaded and conquered these countries, Jews across Europe found themselves trapped and with nowhere else to turn.

Thinking It Over

1. What was the impact of Kristallnacht on the Jewish community in Germany?
2. Why do you think the Nazis targeted Jewish synagogues for destruction?

GOING TO THE SOURCE

Facing Hatred During Kristallnacht

Frederic Zeller was a Jewish boy in Berlin during the 1930s. He faced a great deal of persecution during those years. He and his sister were sent to England before World War II began. In 1957, Zeller moved to the United States. Below is a description of some of his experiences during Kristallnacht.

Mother was relieved to see me back, but tears were running down her cheeks.

"They're looting the Hochmann store. They have no shame. The poor woman will have nothing left..."

"Yes, I just saw them. I'll empty her [store] window and take the stuff to the back, if there's anything left..."

I ran down, crossed the street, interrupted a woman in the process of putting her hand into the window, and saying "Please" climbed over the glass...into the narrow window space. The woman pulled her arm back hastily, looked embarrassed, then huffed, then ran.

People stopped and watched me curiously. It must have seemed strange: a thin, gangling kid clearing the window all on his own. Some people looked sulky, others sad or shocked. And then there were those who gloated. What hateful faces. Suddenly I became aware of a thin, tall, gray-haired man....He was screaming at me, and in such a rage, I could hardly understand a word. What had I done, I wondered. Had I dropped some glass on him? A few words stood out:

"Jewpigs...murderers...filthy cowards...killed...good German!"

And all the while he was holding, with both hands, a shabby, leather briefcase, folded in two—threatening to smash it into the large jagged glass spikes next to and above my head....I knew that if I showed fear, flinched or jumped back, he would strike. I knew this for sure.

I saw the hate-distorted face of the man . . . [and] the person next to him, intercepting him in slow motion. And I heard the words...

"Stop it, he's only a child." I felt my face freeze into nonexpression. I emptied myself of fear. Turning . . . turning my back to the threat. Turning my back to him....Starting to work again, emptying the window. Numb. I felt nothing.

> From Frederic Zeller, *When Time Ran Out:*
> *Coming of Age in the Third Reich.* New York:
> Permanent Press, 1989, pp. 138–139.

1. Why did Frederic run down to the store?
2. Why was the gray-haired man screaming at Frederic?

Case Study Review

Identifying Main Ideas

1. Why were so many Germans ready to listen to Hitler's message of hate?
2. How did the Nuremberg laws push Jews out of German society?
3. Why was the SS such an important organization in Nazi Germany?

Working Together

Form a group with four classmates. Together you will create an illustrated time line of the events leading up to Kristallnacht. Assign each person in your group a section of Case Study 2. Next, have each person review their section and write down dates on which key events occurred. Review your group's events and choose at least seven to include on your time line. Then, choose two or three events to illustrate. Finally, draw your time line on a large sheet of paper and display it in the classroom.

Active Learning

Conducting an Interview Work with a classmate. Review the notes you took while reading this case study. Decide what type of person you would like to interview. For example, you may interview a Jew or non-Jew, a man, a woman, or a child. Then, make a list of at least ten questions to ask this person. Prepare the answers that you think the person would give. Review the questions and answers with your teacher. Finally, perform your interview with your partner for the class.

Lessons for Today

Joseph Goebbels, the Nazi Chief of Propaganda, believed in big lies. Goebbels once wrote that "a little lie may not be believed by all, but a big lie, if repeated with sufficient frequency, will eventually take deep root in the minds of the uninformed masses." Do you agree that people will begin to believe a lie if it is repeated enough? Can you think of an example? How can we prevent "big lies" from being believed?

What Might You Have Done?

Imagine that you lived in Germany in the 1930s. After hearing Hitler's ideas about race and seeing Nazi propaganda posters, you and a group of your friends have decided to start a campaign against Hitler. What types of media would you use to reach people? You may decide to use radio, magazines, posters, or pamphlets. Create a sample of the type of method you choose to use. For example, if you decide to use posters, draw a poster with words and images that communicate your message.

CRITICAL THINKING

Questioning Unfair Attitudes, Opinions, and Beliefs

You may have encountered people who have attitudes, opinions, and beliefs that are unfair or harmful to others. It often takes courage to question those attitudes, opinions, and beliefs. To do so, you have to listen to and honestly consider other points of view.

By honestly considering other points of view, you remain fair. Being fair-minded helps you to recognize the truth.

Consider the way that the German people reacted to Adolf Hitler's racist ideas. In his book, *Mein Kampf*, Hitler outlined his ridiculous theories of racial superiority and anti-Semitism. He blamed all of Germany's problems on the Jews. At first, most Germans rejected Hitler as a fanatic—someone with far-fetched ideas. *Mein Kampf* did not sell much at all.

As hard times wore Germans down, however, many people saw Hitler's ideas as an easy way to explain their misfortune. Most German people stopped looking at things in a fair way. Suddenly Hitler's book became a best-seller. In 1930, over 50,000 copies of *Mein Kampf* were sold. In 1932, 90,000 copies were sold. Most people did not even read the book. Instead, they blindly accepted Hitler's ideas about the Jews and hoped he would solve Germany's problems. They did not stop to question his—or their own—opinions and beliefs about the Jews.

Think about the ways in which you decide if attitudes, opinions, and beliefs are fair or unfair. Then, answer the questions below.

1. If most people around you share an opinion on an issue, why is difficult to question or disagree with them?

2. When is it a good idea to question or disagree with others?

3. Is it ever a good idea *not* to question or disagree with others? When and why?

4. Why is it difficult to reconsider or question your own attitudes, opinions, and beliefs?

I used to believe	Now I believe	I changed my mind because

5. Have you ever changed your belief about something? Copy the chart above into your notebook. Fill in the boxes to describe what you used to believe and what you now believe.

6. Did it take courage to change your attitude or belief? Why or why not?

7. What would make a person think it was right for the Jews to be driven from their homes, lose their property, and even lose their lives?

8. Why do you think more people did not try to help the Jews as persecution of them grew after 1933?

DISCUSSION

Between 1933 and 1939, the Nazis passed laws that took away the civil rights of Jews in Germany. Jews were not considered citizens of Germany. They could not vote. They could not own property. They could not be paid wages as employees. They could not operate businesses. Signs saying "Jews not welcomed" were posted in theaters, restaurants, hotels, and shops. In public parks, Jews could sit on benches marked "for Jews only." These laws were examples of anti-Semitism. The Jews were discriminated against solely because of their religion and race.

What are your beliefs about people's rights? Should everyone have the same rights, regardless of ethnicity, gender, or religion? What are the reasons for your opinions?

Armed storm troopers force Jewish women and children from their homes in the Warsaw Ghetto to Nazi concentration camps.

THE WARSAW GHETTO UPRISING: JEWS FIGHT BACK

CRITICAL QUESTIONS
- What effect did ghetto life have on Jews during the Holocaust?
- In what ways can people resist oppression and persecution?

TERMS TO KNOW
- Passover
- Einsatzgruppen
- Star of David
- Judenrat

ACTIVE LEARNING

As you read this case study, note how different people reacted to ghetto life. After you are finished reading, you will be asked to write several journal or diary entries from the point of view of a ghetto resident. Look for the Active Learning boxes as you read about the Warsaw Ghetto Uprising.

Monday, April 19, 1943, was the eve of **Passover.** Passover is the holiday when Jews celebrate their liberation from slavery in Egypt over 3,000 years ago. In Warsaw, Poland in 1943, the Jews had little to celebrate. Thousands of Jews were struggling to stay alive in a ghetto set up by the Nazis. Despite terrible conditions, the Jews in the Warsaw Ghetto had prepared for the holiday as best they could.

There would be no time to celebrate Passover that Monday night, however. For months the Jews of the ghetto had been secretly preparing for something else. They planned to strike back at the Nazis who had been persecuting them since 1939. They had been gathering what weapons they could find for the attack.

By 1943, almost 90 percent of the 450,000 people forced into the Warsaw Ghetto were dead. Those who had managed to survive ghetto life were the hardiest of Warsaw's Jews. They were mostly young people whom the Nazis forced into labor. Despite their youth, they had witnessed unbelievable horrors. They also knew they did not have long to live.

Fighting the Nazis was an extremely difficult task. The German army had tanks, flamethrowers, cannons, and other sophisticated weaponry. The Jewish fighters had homemade gasoline bombs, hand grenades, a few rifles, and one or two submachine guns. Other than that, they had only their courage and will.

For 28 days, these young Jewish men and women fought the powerful German army. The young Jewish fighters numbered fewer than 1,000. Many of them were teenagers. Their leader, Mordechai Anielewicz, was only 24 years old.

Simcha Ratajzer was on guard during the predawn blackness of April 19. Later, he described what he saw that morning.

At 4:00 in the morning we saw a column of Nazis moving toward the central ghetto. Some thousands were marching without end. After that, some tanks go by, armored vehicles, light cannons, and hundreds of people of the SS units on bicycles. "They move as if they are going to war," I said...and I suddenly felt how weak we were. What am I, and what is our strength against an armed and well-equipped army, against tanks and armored cars, and we have merely pistols and at best, hand grenades.

How had life for the Jews of Warsaw come to this? Why had they been forced to live in a horrible ghetto? In this case study, you will learn about the events that led to the Warsaw Ghetto Uprising.

1 The Nazis Come to Poland

On September 1, 1939, the German army invaded Poland. With this event, Great Britain and France declared war on Germany. World War II had begun. The Germans took control of Warsaw, Poland's capital, in less than a month. A few weeks later, the fighting in Poland was over. Most of the country was under German control.

The Einsatzgruppen

The conquest of Poland placed about two million Polish Jews under Nazi control. A secret agreement between Germany and the Soviet Union gave a large section of eastern Poland to the Soviet Union. About 1 million Jews lived in this Soviet-controlled territory. An additional 350,000 Jews fled the Germans into the Soviet-controlled areas.

Before the end of 1939, over 120,000 Jews were dead. Some died as soldiers in the Polish army. Others were killed along with their non-Jewish neighbors in German bombing attacks on Polish cities. Many Jews were deliberately murdered by special SS units assigned to kill Jews. These units were called the **Einsatzgruppen.** After 1941, the Einsatzgruppen would murder nearly 1.5 million Jews in the Soviet Union.

In 1940, German troops overran most of the countries of Western Europe. This brought hundreds of thousands of additional Jews under Nazi control.

New Horrors

In Poland, the Germans immediately began to terrorize the entire population. However, the Jews were singled out for the most brutal treatment.

The Germans expelled thousands of Jews living near the new Soviet/German border. The Germans forced the Jews to leave Poland and flee to the Soviet Union. Entire towns were emptied of Jews. Jewish families had lived in these towns for hundreds of years.

In one town, 4,000 Jews were driven from their homes. They were forbidden to take any of their belongings. The Germans shot many of them as they walked toward a river where Soviet territory began. A witness recalled:

On the bank of the river Gestapo men were waiting and driving people into a...raft of two unbalanced boards, from which women and children fell into the river....Near the bank women stood in the water, holding their children above their heads and crying for help, to which the Gestapo men answered by shooting. Blood, masses of floating corpses. It is impossible to describe the despair...of people in such a situation.

The Polish Jews who were not immediately expelled from their homes suffered terribly as well. German soldiers hunted down religious Jews and cut off their beards. They beat up Jews on the streets. German soldiers raided Jewish homes, taking furniture, cash, and other valuable items. They kidnapped Jews and sent them into forced labor.

By December 1939, all Jews were ordered to wear the yellow **Star of David** on their

During the Holocaust, Jews in Nazi-controlled Europe endured endless suffering and humiliation. Here, a Jewish son is forced to cut off his father's beard as amused German soldiers watch.

clothing. The six-pointed Star of David is a symbol of the Jewish people. The star allowed the Nazis to immediately identify Jews.

The Nazis continued to terrorize Jews in village after village. A woman described what happened in her village shortly after the Germans arrived in 1939.

> *The Germans forced their way into a private house, where Jews were praying, and ordered those present to go out and run; then they ordered "halt," but several Jews did not hear and carried on running; they then opened fire and killed five or six of them.*

On Yom Kippur (the Day of Atonement), the holiest day of the Jewish year, the Germans burned down two large synagogues. A witness recalled:

> *The fire spread to some private houses. The Jews threw their possessions out of the window and were thereupon robbed by a mob of non-Jews....Then hunting expeditions on Jewish houses took place. They caught 350*

Jews and put some of them into a military barracks and others into [a] factory....Those who were taken, or caught in the street, were beaten up and humiliated endlessly.

Thinking It Over

1. What did the Nazis do to the Jews living near the Soviet border?
2. Why were Jews forced to wear a Star of David on their clothing?

2 The Move to the Ghettos

While the persecution of Jews continued, the Nazis were planning something even worse.

Before the war, the Polish city of Lodz (looj) had a large and thriving Jewish community in which leading artists, musicians, and scientists lived. With the German takeover, the Jews of Lodz were herded into a crowded ghetto. Few of Lodz's Jews survived the war.

Late in September 1939, a top SS officer named Reinhard Heydrich sent a notice to his forces in Poland. It called for "planned total measures" for dealing with the Jews.

The first of these measures was to gather Poland's Jews into ghettos. The ghettos were places to hold the Jews until the Nazis thought of a "final solution" to their "Jewish problem." In 1941, the Nazis decided what the "final solution" would be: the extermination of all Jews.

The Nazis began forcing Jews into ghettos late in October 1939. The first large ghetto was set up in the city of Lodz early in 1940. The Warsaw Ghetto was established in October of that year.

As the Jews were herded into ghettos, they were brutally treated. One woman described how in her town all the Jews had to leave by March 5, 1940. She recalled that "every day one could see [Jews] in the snow-covered streets. Caravans [long lines] of people carrying on their backs pieces of furniture, bags, and suitcases."

In October 1940 in Warsaw, a young Jewish mother named Tosha Bialer watched people moving in "an endless stream." They were "pushing, wheeling, dragging all their belongings from every part of the city into one small section."

In the narrow streets of the ghettos, people went from house to house looking for a place to live. Many were unsuccessful. Over and over Bialer heard people ask, "Have you room?" Bialer recalled:

> Children wandered, lost and crying, parents ran…seeking them, their cries drowned in the tremendous hubbub of half a million uprooted people.

By 1942, almost all Polish Jews were in ghettos. Only a few who found hiding places elsewhere escaped ghetto life.

The Warsaw Ghetto

Conditions in the Warsaw Ghetto were terrible from the first day. In November, the ghetto was sealed off from the rest of the city by a brick wall. The Germans had forced the Jews to build and pay for the wall themselves. German police guarded every opening in the wall.

Overcrowding was an immediate problem in the ghetto. The Germans crammed one-third of Warsaw's population into less than 2.4 percent of its area. Fifteen or more people now lived in a space where four people had lived before.

The Germans purposely limited the amount of food that could be brought into the ghetto. They wanted the Jews to slowly starve to death. The official ration for a Jew was 800 calories a day, half of what a Pole outside the ghetto was rationed and much too little to survive on.

In their desperate struggle to find food, Jews turned to smuggling. Among the best smugglers were very young children. They were small enough to slip through holes in the ghetto wall or crawl through sewers that led out of the ghetto. Sometimes they hid by the ghetto gates and sneaked through the gates when the guards were not looking.

If the children were successful, they might find some food for themselves and their families.

A Good Movie to See

Lodz Ghetto, The Jewish Heritage Project, distributed by Pacific Arts Video, Los Angeles, California, 1992. A PBS Home Video.

Watch this film and you will get a sense of what it was like to live in a Jewish ghetto during the Holocaust. The film combines passages from diaries kept by people trapped in the ghetto with film footage from the Holocaust era and today.

However, Nazi guards often caught and shot them. The people in the ghetto were so hungry that not even the threat of death stopped them from smuggling food.

Hunger, overcrowding, and unsanitary conditions led to the spread of disease. The Germans allowed almost no medicine into the ghetto. Efforts to smuggle in medicine were rarely successful. During the first year of the ghetto, over 43,000 people starved to death. Another 15,000 died of a deadly disease called typhus. Other diseases also killed many people. Among the worst was tuberculosis, a lung disease.

The Nazis quickly achieved the horrible results they wanted. In 1941, a report from the German army called the conditions in the ghetto "catastrophic." The report said, "Dead bodies from those who collapsed from lack of strength are lying in the streets."

A Polish visitor to the ghetto described the people he saw. Starvation had turned the Jews into "nightmare figures, ghosts of former human beings." After only one hour in the ghetto, he reported:

> I no longer look at people; when I hear groaning and sobbing I go over to the other side of the road; when I see something wrapped in rags, shivering with cold, stretched out on the ground I turn away and do not want to look....I can't. It's become too much for me.

Thinking It Over

1. Why did the Nazis create ghettos?
2. What were the main causes of death among Jews in the ghettos?

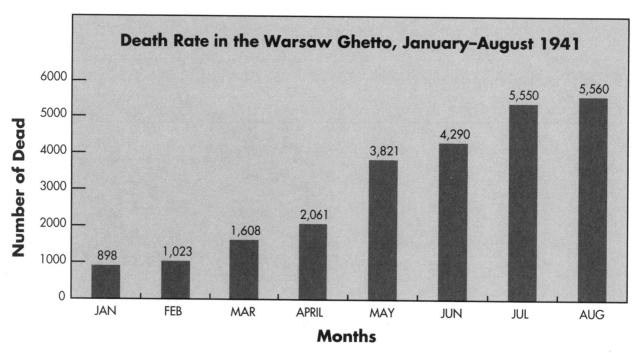

Source: Rogasky, Barbara, *Smoke and Ashes: The Story of the Holocaust*, p. 42.

Trapped in the Warsaw Ghetto, Jews died at an alarming rate through 1941. In which months of 1941 did the number of deaths increase from the previous month?

3 Governing the Ghetto

The Nazis appointed a group of Jews to govern each ghetto. This group was called the Jewish Council, or **Judenrat**.

The Judenrat

It is important to remember that the Judenrat in Warsaw and every other ghetto had no power. All Jewish Councils operated directly under the orders of the Nazis. If they refused Nazi orders, they were punished severely.

Shmuel Zygelboim, a member of Warsaw's Judenrat, described the council's first meeting with the Nazis.

> *A Gestapo officer…came to the meeting and delivered a speech as if he were speaking to criminals. He ordered the Judenrat to stand while listening. He said that the fate of the Jews and of the Judenrat was in the hands of the Gestapo. The Judenrat was not to approach any other Nazi officer. No discussions.*

The chairman of the Warsaw Judenrat was an engineer named Adam Czerniakow. He served in that post for almost two years. At the first meeting of the Judenrat, he showed its 24 members a small bottle he kept in his desk. It contained 24 poison pills.

The Judenrat tried to meet the Nazi demands while protecting and caring for the Jews of Warsaw. It ran soup kitchens for the poorest people of the ghetto. It tried to provide heat, water, jobs, and other services to the people. It ran schools and provided religious and cultural activities.

The Judenrat in Warsaw and in every ghetto attempted to keep alive as many Jews as possible. It tried to protect the Jewish community and to avoid Nazi orders whenever it could. However, it met Nazi demands when there was absolutely no choice.

Despite the good intentions of the members of the Judenrat, they could not save the Jews after 1941. At that point, the Nazis had come up with the "final solution." They decided to murder the entire Jewish population. Despite the horrors they witnessed and experienced over the years, many Jews did not believe that this was the goal of the Nazis.

When Judenrat officials found out about the death camps where many Jews had already perished, they still could not believe the Nazis planned to kill *all* the Jews. The ghettos were cut off from the outside world. There were no newspapers or radios allowed. All kinds of rumors spread. No one living in the ghetto knew what to believe. So the Judenrat continued their struggle to protect Jewish lives.

In July 1942, Adam Czerniakow was given an order to gather Jews for what the Nazis called "resettlement." Czerniakow realized that these people were to be sent to the death camps. Rather than carry out the order, he left it unsigned and committed suicide.

Preserving Dignity

Emmanuel Ringelblum was 39 years old in 1939. He was a leader in Poland's Jewish community. Ringelblum was a historian and teacher. He kept a careful record of everything he saw in the Warsaw Ghetto.

Even locked in the ghetto, the Jews of Warsaw continued their pursuit of education. Here, at a ghetto school, boys study poetry in Yiddish, the language most of them knew best.

Ringelblum wrote how, despite terrible conditions, people struggled to keep their dignity. As Ringelblum put it, "We did not lose our human characteristics. Our minds are as busy as they were before the war."

One way people kept their minds busy was by reading. Reading allowed Jews to escape the ghetto walls in their imagination. The books they read gave them hope for a better future.

The Jews in Warsaw and other ghettos did other things to maintain as normal a life as possible. The Germans forbade most of these activities. They therefore had to be carried out in secret. Among the most important activities were classes for children. In the Warsaw Ghetto, there was a special children's library and classes for medical students.

Groups met to read and discuss important writers. A secret group called the Jewish Cultural Organization organized lectures and other programs. Plays and concerts took place despite the hardship and terror of ghetto life.

The Jews of Warsaw continued to practice their faith. They held secret religious instruction and services, and they continued to celebrate Jewish holidays.

Many Jews hoped to move to the United States some day. There was a large group that studied English.

Perhaps the most amazing fact about the Warsaw Ghetto was the lack of serious crime there. Despite scanty food and miserable living conditions, the Jews did not attack one another. Until the deportations to the death camps began in 1942, there were no murders committed in the Warsaw Ghetto.

Active Learning: What were the different ways in which Jews resisted the Nazis? Make a list of all the things that Jews did to preserve their traditions and their dignity. Be sure to include this information in your journal or diary.

Thinking It Over

1. What was the Judenrat?
2. How did the Jews in the Warsaw Ghetto preserve their dignity?

4 The Warsaw Ghetto Uprising

During April 1942, the people in the Warsaw Ghetto first heard reports about the death camps. Many of them could not believe it. At that point, even Adam Czerniakow thought the reports were exaggerated.

The Jewish Fighting Organization

The younger leaders of the Jewish community believed the reports. They soon found out that they were correct. In July, the Germans began deporting Jews from Warsaw to the death camp at Treblinka. By September, they had deported over 300,000 Jews to the camp. Officially, only about 55,000 Jews remained alive in the Warsaw Ghetto. Thousands of others went into hiding rather than report for deportation.

The younger leaders set up the Jewish Fighting Organization in July. However, preparing to fight the Nazis proved very difficult. The Jews in the ghetto were isolated. It was almost impossible to get weapons. They received almost no help from Polish people outside the ghetto. Still, the organization forged ahead.

By the end of 1942, the fighting organization had pushed the Judenrat aside and had taken control of the Warsaw Ghetto. It raised money and was able to buy some weapons outside the ghetto.

On January 18, 1943, the fighting organization fought its first battle with German troops. The Jewish fighters attacked Nazi troops that were rounding up hundreds of Jews from the ghetto for deportation. During the short battle, the Jews that were to be deported scattered and escaped from the Nazis.

However, most of the Jewish fighters were killed in the battle. Mordechai Anielewicz and other leaders decided to be better prepared before trying a full-scale uprising.

Four days later, the fighting organization announced to the people of the Warsaw Ghetto:

Jewish masses! The hour is close. You must be prepared to resist....Our slogan should be: We should all be ready to die as human beings.

"I Have Been A Witness..."

On April 19, 1943, the Germans sent 2,000 heavily armed soldiers into the Warsaw Ghetto. This date marked the start of the Warsaw Ghetto Uprising. This time, the Jewish fighters were prepared. They had fortified themselves in places throughout the ghetto.

The fighting began at about 6 A.M. The Germans used their tanks, armored cars, cannons, and flamethrowers. The Jews fought back with their guns, rifles, and homemade gasoline bombs.

Several times the Jews were able to surprise and attack the Germans. In one battle, Jews with homemade bombs managed to destroy a German tank. Jewish fighters got away from the Germans by escaping over the rooftops.

After a day of fighting, the Germans retreated from the ghetto. A young woman named Zivia Lubetkin recalled "the wonder and the miracle" of how the "German heroes retreated, afraid and terrorized from Jewish bombs and hand grenades, homemade."

However, the Germans came back the next day under a new commander. Once again the fighting was fierce. The Germans decided on a new strategy. Instead of fighting

After four weeks of bitter fighting, the Warsaw Ghetto was in ruins, and a few Jewish survivors were flushed from their positions. Here, a German officer captures a survivor from a hidden bunker.

house-to-house, they bombed the ghetto and burned it down.

Inch by inch, the Jewish fighters had to retreat. Marek Edelman described what happened to his group as they fled the flames.

> *The asphalt melts under [our] feet....The heat from the paving stones burns the soles of [our] shoes. One after another we flee through the flames, from building to building, yard to yard. There is no air left to breathe....Burning wooden beams fall on us.*

Slowly the Germans used their overwhelming power to advance. On May 8, they took the headquarters of the Jewish Fighting Organization. The Germans used poison gas to kill the Jewish fighters inside who refused to surrender. Anielewicz and several leaders of the uprising committed suicide rather than be taken alive by the Nazis.

Two days before his death, Mordechai Anielewicz wrote a letter to one of his commanders. Anielewicz knew the end was near. Yet, he wrote:

> *What really matters is the dream...has come true. Jewish self defense in Warsaw has become a fact....I have been a witness to the magnificent heroic struggle of the Jewish fighters.*

The fighting did not end until May 16. The Germans had planned to crush the Jews in three days. Instead, it took them four weeks. By then the entire ghetto lay in ruins. A few Jews managed to escape. The Nazis deported the Jews they captured to the Treblinka death camp.

The Warsaw Ghetto Uprising remains an important event for many reasons. It was the first significant armed revolt against the Nazis by civilians. It shocked the Nazis and became an inspiration for Jews elsewhere in Europe. Finally, the Warsaw Ghetto Uprising serves as an example of the courage and strength that people can find even in the worst of times.

Thinking It Over

1. Why was it difficult for the Jews to prepare to fight the Nazis?
2. Why was Mordechai Anielewicz proud of what he and the other Jewish fighters did?

GOING TO THE SOURCE

The Warsaw Ghetto Uprising

Young leaders in the Warsaw Ghetto formed the Jewish Fighting Organization in 1942. They knew that the chances of defeating the Nazis were very slim. But as one ghetto leader put it, "We must resist. Young and old alike must oppose the enemy." The fighting organization fought an all-out battle with the German army from April 19 to May 16, 1943. The picture below shows Jewish captives being marched out of the Warsaw Ghetto by the Nazis at the end of the uprising.

Jewish men, women, and children were forced to march through the streets of Warsaw on their way to trains bound for Nazi death camps. After the war, a few Nazi leaders were put on trial for war crimes. This photograph and others shown in this case study were used to convict them.

1. What are the ages of the Jewish captives?
2. What is the condition of the buildings in the ghetto?

Case Study Review

Identifying Main Ideas

1. What were conditions like in the ghettos that the Nazis set up?
2. How did Jews try to maintain their dignity while living under terrible conditions in the ghetto?
3. What did the Jewish Fighting Organization mean when it announced that Jews should be ready to "die like human beings"?

Working Together

Form a small group. Use the information in this case study and other resources to create a visual memorial of the Warsaw Ghetto Uprising. Decide what images you would like to show in your memorial. Then use pictures from magazines or newspapers or your own drawings to portray these images. First, draw a sketch to show how you wish to organize the images in your memorial. Then, use a large piece of paper to create it.

 ## Active Learning

Writing a Journal or Diary Entry Review the notes you took when you read the case study. Imagine that you were a witness to what happened in the Warsaw Ghetto. Write two or three journal or diary entries telling about daily life or relating the details of an important event like the Warsaw Ghetto Uprising. Share your entries with a partner and discuss how to make them more realistic.

Lessons for Today

During the Nazi era, Protestant minister Martin Neimoeller said, "First they came for the Communists, but I wasn't a Communist—so I didn't object. Then they came for the Socialists, but I wasn't a Socialist—so I didn't object. Then they came for the trade union leaders, but I wasn't a union leader—so I didn't object. Then they came for the Jews, but I wasn't a Jew—so I didn't object. Then they came for me—and there was no one left to object."

What message was this minister trying to relate? Do you think people feel this way today? Explain.

What Might You Have Done?

Emmanuel Ringelblum organized activities to help the Jews of the Warsaw Ghetto keep what he called their "human characteristics." What activities might you have suggested given the conditions of the ghetto?

Nazi Reports on the Warsaw Ghetto Uprising

Critical readers pay attention to an author's choice of information. They consider what this choice may tell about the author's point of view. Critical readers try to determine whether they are reading a fair and balanced account or one that is biased.

In this case study, you have read about the Warsaw Ghetto Uprising. You are aware of what the Nazis did to the Jews in the Warsaw Ghetto before the uprising occurred. You are also aware of the Nazi attitude toward the Jews in general and their policy of exterminating all Jews.

Read the excerpts below from *The Jews of Warsaw: 1939–1943 Ghetto, Underground, Revolt* by Yisrael Guttman. The first is from the reports by General Jurgen Stroop. Stroop was the commander of German forces in the Warsaw Ghetto Uprising. The second excerpt is a public announcement by Dr. Ludwig Fischer. Fischer was the Nazi governor of the Warsaw district. The statement was directed to the Polish population of Warsaw.

Report of Jurgen Stroop:

> Last night patrol units in the ghetto reported that they did not come up against Jews, except on rare occasions….In the exchange of fire that took place during the afternoon hours—when the thugs again fought with Molotov cocktails [gasoline-filled bottles], revolvers, and homemade hand grenades—after the gang was destroyed, one of the policemen…was wounded by a bullet in his right thigh. The last block that remains intact…was searched a second time and then destroyed by a special commando unit. Toward evening the synagogue in the Jewish cemetery, the mortuary room, and all the surrounding buildings were blown up or set to torch….

> One hundred and eighty Jews, thugs, and the scum of humanity were killed. The Grand Aktion ended at [8:15 p.m.] with the demolition of the Warsaw Synagogue.

Announcement by Ludwig Fischer:

> Lately there have been a series of murderous attacks in the city of Warsaw. The same force stands behind these attacks as those who hope one day to bring to this country the bloody rule of the Bolsheviks [communists]. Everyone's task is to frustrate

The Language of Thinking

Critical readers identify key ideas while reading. Then they look for information that supports these ideas. Critical readers also consider an author's perspective, or point of view, and the author's purpose. For example, they ask themselves: Is the author simply presenting information, or is the author also trying to persuade me to think a certain way?

the...Communist and Jewish agents. Every Jew and Bolshevik who is still alive and free is the most dangerous enemy of the population....Whoever informs the authorities where such a Jewish or Communist agent moves about freely, is thereby fulfilling his obvious duty to himself and his neighbors.

Copy the chart below into your notebook. Use the chart and the questions below to help you organize your thoughts on one of the selections you just read. In the circle of the chart, summarize the author's perspective of the Warsaw Ghetto Uprising and the Jews. Then in the boxes around the circle, write the specific facts, details, or reasons that the author uses to support this view. After you have completed the chart for one selection, repeat the process for the second selection.

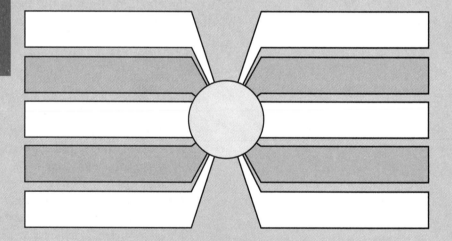

1. What words does Stroop use to portray the Jews? With which group does Fischer link the Jews?

2. Fischer made his statement to hundreds of thousands of Poles in Warsaw. What does he want them to think about the Jews and the Warsaw Ghetto Uprising? What have you learned from the case study about the goals of the uprising? How does your knowledge of the uprising compare with Fischer's view?

Day after day, inmates at slave labor camps were forced to do the most brutal work. Here, prisoners at the Mauthausen camp haul heavy cart loads of earth.

AUSCHWITZ: DEATH CAMP, CONCENTRATION CAMP, SLAVE LABOR CAMP

CRITICAL QUESTIONS

- How did Nazi anti-Semitism lead to the construction of the various camps?
- How did the plan to exterminate the Jews weaken the German army?

TERMS TO KNOW

- Auschwitz
- Final Solution
- gas chamber
- crematorium
- Zyklon B
- sterilize

ACTIVE LEARNING

After you read this case study, you will be asked to create a map that includes the names and locations of the Nazi death camps. Choose two or three classmates to work with. As you read the case study, take notes on the countries, cities, and other locations mentioned. Look for the Active Learning boxes located throughout the case study.

It was August 28, 1942. A freight train crowded with over 1,000 Jewish prisoners left Paris and headed eastward. Several hundred prisoners were children under the age of 16. Many similar freight trains were making their way across Europe in the summer of 1942. They were bound for Poland. There the Nazis had built six death camps.

There were no comforts on these trains. There were no seats. A bucket of water and another bucket that served as a toilet was all there was. The windows were blocked by barbed wire. Cars that might have held 40 people were crammed with 100.

Albert Hollender was on the train that left Paris on August 28. The journey took three days. Inside, Hollender remembered how he and the others could hardly move or breathe.

Piled up in freight cars, unable to bend or budge, breathless, crushed by one's neighbor's every move, this was already hell.

Finally, the train arrived at its destination. But there was no relief for the prisoners. As Hollender described:

After several days and several nights, the doors were opened. We arrived worn out, dehydrated, with many ill. A newborn baby, snatched from its mother's arms, was thrown against a column. The mother, crazed from pain, began to scream. The SS man struck her violently with the butt end of his weapon.... Her eyes haggard, with fearful screams, her beautiful hair became tinted with her own blood. She was struck down with a bullet in the head.

The train from Paris had arrived at **Auschwitz** (AUSH-vits). It was the largest of the Nazi death camps. Of the Jews who came to Auschwitz on that train, Hollender was one of only eight Jews to survive. That August alone the Nazis murdered over 400,000 Jews.

In this case study, you will read how the Nazis planned the destruction of the Jews. You will find out how the Nazis built Auschwitz and other camps. You will learn what it was like for the inmates of Auschwitz. You may find that this story is a difficult one to read. Keep in mind, however, that it is a story that must be told.

1 The Final Solution

During the summer of 1941, Rudolf Hoess received an order to come to SS headquarters in Berlin. Hoess was the SS officer in charge of Auschwitz. At the time, Auschwitz was not yet a death camp. It was still a concentration camp where Jews were detained and often worked to death. Hoess was to come to Berlin to meet with Heinrich Himmler, the head of the SS.

Behind the German forces that invaded the Soviet Union were the extermination squads of the Einsatzgruppen. Here a German officer executes an innocent citizen. His crime: he was Jewish.

Himmler had important news. He said that Adolf Hitler had ordered the **"Final Solution** to the Jewish problem." The SS had the job of carrying it out. The Final Solution was the term the Nazis used to refer to their plans to completely exterminate the Jewish people.

Even before Hitler ordered the Final Solution, the Nazis had started the mass killing of Jews. On June 22, Nazi Germany invaded the Soviet Union. Several million Jews lived there. Among them were over one million Jews who lived in the territory that had been part of Poland before 1939. (See Case Study 3.)

The German army marched into the Soviet Union. Behind it came the Einsatzgruppen, the unit of the SS assigned to kill Jews. The Einsatzgruppen carried out the mass murder of Jews in the newly conquered areas. After Jews were shot, their bodies were buried in mass graves.

The worst massacre occurred at Babi Yar outside the city of Kiev in Ukraine. The Germans, with help from local Ukrainian police, shot over 33,000 Jews in two days.

The Einsatzgruppen eventually murdered nearly 1.4 million Jews. However, they noticed serious problems with their killing methods. Many of the men who did the killing became physically or mentally sick. The men couldn't bear to face their victims. Also, burying the victims in mass graves left behind evidence of the horrible crime.

The Nazis needed a way to carry out the Final Solution that did not bring killers and their victims face to face. They also needed a more efficient way to kill people and dispose of their bodies. Himmler and the SS were told to solve these "problems."

The Wannsee Conference

On January 10, 1942, 15 high-ranking Nazi officials met in a suburb of Berlin called Wannsee. The conference was called by Reinhard Heydrich, one of the highest-ranking SS officials. Its purpose was to plan the complete extermination of the Jews.

Heydrich said that plans had to be made for "evacuation of Jews to the East." This "evacuation" really meant deportation to death camps. When Heydrich mentioned the Final Solution, everyone there knew he meant the killing of all the Jews in Europe.

Present at the meeting was an SS lieutenant colonel named Adolf Eichmann. Eichmann recalled that at the conference the officials "spoke about killing, about liquidation, about extermination." Eichmann would rise high in the Nazi regime. By 1942, he was in charge of what the SS called its "Jewish Office." After Wannsee, Eichmann took charge of transporting millions of Jews from all over Europe to the Nazi death camps in Poland. He was one of the most important Nazi officials that directly participated in the extermination of the Jews. (See Case Study 8 for more on Eichmann.)

Who Is a Jew?

Nazi officials could not decide exactly whom they considered a Jew. According to the Nuremberg Laws, any person with at least three Jewish grandparents was a Jew. But what about people with two or only one Jewish grandparent?

This question was of great concern to the Nazis. Their fierce anti-Semitism arose from an obsession with the "purity of German blood" and perfecting the Aryan race. It made no difference to them that their theories about race had no scientific basis. They simply wanted to clearly identify—and destroy—their enemy.

The Nazis never did determine how to classify people who had one or two Jewish grandparents, but they had many theories. For example, Heydrich believed that some people with two Jewish grandparents were Jewish if they had an "especially unfavorable appearance in racial terms." In other words, certain people might be considered Jewish if the Nazis did not like how they looked.

The Nazis also classified some of these people as Jews if they participated in certain activities, such as attending synagogue. The

Nazis said that the way people acted could make them members of a certain race.

In the end, most people with one or two Jewish grandparents were not considered Jews. However, some were sent to the death camps anyway.

Thinking It Over

1. What did the Nazis mean by the term "Final Solution"?
2. Why did Heydrich bring together Nazi officials at the Wannsee conference?

2 The Nazi Death Machine

After the Wannsee conference, the Nazis began to put the Final Solution into operation. They built a gigantic death machine that consisted of deportation to death camps and methods of mass murder. The Nazi death machine was the result of careful planning and the use of modern technology. Everything from the location of the death camps to the methods of murder was carefully worked out. Using Germany's scientists, businessmen, engineers, and officials, the Nazis built a modern and efficient way to eliminate the Jews.

At camps throughout the territory under their control, the Nazis set out to exterminate Europe's Jews. Why were most death camps and concentration camps located in Germany and Poland? Why do you think Spain, Switzerland, Ireland, Sweden, and Turkey are not shaded on this map?

The Death Camps

The core of the Nazi death machine consisted of six death camps. All of them were located in Poland near major cities. Each one was on a major railroad line so its victims could easily be transported there.

One reason for putting the camps in Poland was secrecy. In Poland, the SS was in total control. They could conceal their activities more easily in Poland than in Germany or in Western Europe.

Another reason was the large number of Jews in Poland. Polish Jews would not have to be transported to camps far away.

The largest death camp was Auschwitz near the city of Cracow. You will read about Auschwitz later in this case study. The other death camps were Chelmno, Treblinka, Sobibor, Maidanek, and Belzec.

Chelmno was the first death camp to be completed. Located near Lodz, it opened in December 1941. One of the largest Jewish ghettos was in Lodz. Eventually over 300,000 Jews died in Chelmno. Gypsies, Poles, and Soviet prisoners of war were also murdered there.

Treblinka was just east of Warsaw. It began operating on July 23, 1942. About 900,000 Jews were murdered there. Only Auschwitz killed more Jews. Fewer than 100 people taken to Treblinka survived the Holocaust.

On a cold day in January 1943, 1,000 Jews were deported to Treblinka from a nearby village. They traveled on heavy sleds. A Jewish historian named Szymon Datner witnessed this scene.

> There was one man, a very big man physically. . . . He had lived outside in the winter, and he could have escaped. He could have run into the woods.
> But he had in his arms a six-month-old baby—the youngest of his children. And he was together on the sled with his wife and children. His wife . . . said, "Get away, jump, you will survive. What is the use of dying together?" But he said, "No. I will not leave you."

Years later, Datner wrote that in those terrible circumstances the man's decision *not* to

escape was an act of heroism. "I give my full respect before such an act of a simple man. I bow my head in respect before him."

The Sobibor, Belzec, and Maidanek death camps were located near Lublin. A quarter of a million Jews were murdered at Sobibor. In October 1943, the few prisoners still alive at Sobibor staged an uprising. Of the 300 who managed to escape, only 50 survived the Holocaust.

Over half of the 300,000 people murdered at Maidanek were Jews. Many of the others were Poles. The Nazis murdered people from 28 countries and over 50 ethnic groups at Maidanek.

In less than a year, the Nazis murdered over 550,000 Jews at Belzec. Hardly any of the Jews deported there survived. One survivor was Rudolf Reder. He remembered how the trains of death arrived.

> They came every day, without interruption, three times a day. Each train numbered fifty cars, with hundreds of people in each one of them. When the transports arrived at night, the victims of Belzec waited in closed cars until 6 o'clock in the morning. Sometimes the transports were larger and more frequent.

Active Learning: Make a list of all the death camps mentioned in this section. Then locate them on the map on page 54.

Transports of Death

As you have just read, the Nazis used a huge network of trains to transport their victims to the death camps. Over one million employees operated the system. These employees maintained the equipment, set the schedules, and kept the tracks in good repair.

As World War II wore on, the German army needed trains to supply its soldiers. The need grew as Germany and the Axis Powers began losing the war. The Axis Powers were the countries that sided with Germany during the war. Allied bombing raids destroyed many German trains carrying military equipment to the front lines.

But Hitler and the Nazi leaders were so determined to carry out the Final Solution that they made it a priority over supplying German soldiers in the field. Even as Germany was losing the war, the Nazis provided whatever trains were necessary to transport the Jews to the death camps. They allowed nothing to interfere with their plan to exterminate the Jews.

A group of Hungarian Jews is shown upon their arrival in the Auschwitz-Birkenau death camp. The people were locked in cattle cars for two and a half days before their arrival. They emerged from the camps relieved to be alive and unsure of what lay ahead for them in the camp.

Thinking It Over

1. Why did the Nazis locate the death camps near railroad lines?
2. The Nazis decided to use their trains to transport Jews to the death camps, rather than to supply their own troops. What does this tell you about the Nazis' priorities during World War II?

3 The Journey to Auschwitz

The largest of the death camps was Auschwitz. Over one million Jews were murdered there.

Trains came to Auschwitz from all parts of Nazi-occupied Europe. In Western Europe, the trains came from France, Belgium, and Holland. Freight trains packed with Jews came to Auschwitz from Germany and Austria, as well as from Italy.

From Eastern Europe, trains brought Jews from Lithuania, Hungary, and faraway Greece. Death trains bound for Auschwitz also left from small towns in the Soviet Union.

Tens of thousands of Jews died on the journey to the camps. There was little food or water. The closed freight cars became unbearably hot in summer. In winter, they were freezing cold.

Hiding the Truth

The Nazis did all they could to hide the truth from the Jews on the trains. The Nazis made Jews who had just arrived at Auschwitz write postcards home saying, "I am well." Eighteen-year-old Moshe Sandberg and his family were sent to Auschwitz from Hungary. He remembered how the postcards "acted as a sleeping drug." They "came just at the right time . . . to remove any thought of revolt or escape."

The Nazis told the Jews to pack clothing and a few other belongings. They explained to the Jews that they were being resettled or sent to labor camps. The desperate people on the trains were ready to believe anything. They often had no idea what awaited them.

Active Learning: Make a list of the countries from which trains brought Jews to Auschwitz. Locate these countries on the map on page 54.

Arrival at Auschwitz

At Auschwitz, the trains pulled into one of the largest railroad yards in Europe. There were 44 separate tracks. Primo Levi, the famous chemist, was on one of those trains. He was one of the few Auschwitz survivors. The Nazis kept him alive because they needed his skills as a chemist. Levi described his arrival.

> *The climax came suddenly. The door opened with a crash, and the dark echoed with the outlandish orders in that curt, barbaric barking of Germans in command.*
>
> *A vast platform appeared before us, lit up by reflectors. . . . A dozen SS men . . . began to interrogate us . . . [they asked] "How old? Healthy or ill?" And on the basis of the reply they pointed in two different directions.*

Thinking It Over

1. List at least three places in Europe from which trains came to Auschwitz.
2. Why do you think the Nazis misled the Jews about the trip to Auschwitz? Why were Jews willing to believe them?

4 Auschwitz: The Kingdom of Death

Auschwitz was a gigantic complex of three main camps and dozens of smaller camps. It was located in the southwest corner of Poland.

The whole complex covered an area that was miles wide. Thousands of SS men from the "Death's Head" unit guarded the camp. Each Death's Head member wore a skull and crossbones on his uniform.

The original camp at Auschwitz was a concentration camp. It opened on June 14, 1940. After other camps were added, the original concentration camp was called Auschwitz I.

Auschwitz II was the death camp. It was also called Birkenau. The Nazis continually expanded Birkenau until it became a series of camps.

Auschwitz III was a slave labor camp. It had factories that produced materials for the German army. The workers in the factories were slave laborers.

"It Was My Turn..."

The first experience for prisoners at Auschwitz was called "selection." SS officers who were doctors made the selection. Each captive stood before an officer, who waved to the left or to the right.

At this point, families that had managed to stay together were separated often forever. Exhausted from their journey and confused, most people did not understand what was happening.

On the platform at Auschwitz, SS officers barked questions at the prisoners. "How old? Healthy or ill?," one survivor remembered. At this point, families were separated forever. The young, the old, and the ill were sent to the deaths camps. Healthy adults were selected to work as slave laborers.

The very young, and the very old, and those who looked ill were waved in one direction. They were immediately sent to their deaths.

Healthy adults were waved in the other direction. They were "selected" to work as slave laborers. Their hair was then shaved, and they were tattooed with a number. Those selected to work were not in a favorable position. The average life span of a slave laborer at Auschwitz was about three months.

Victor Frankl, an Auschwitz survivor, was a physician. He stood on the platform by the railroad tracks looking at an SS officer "slim and fit in his spotless uniform."

> His right hand was lifted, and with a forefinger of that hand he pointed very leisurely to the right or left.
>
> It was my turn. . . . The SS man looked me over, appeared to hesitate, then put both his hands on my shoulders. I tried very hard to look smart, and he turned my shoulders very slowly to the right, and I moved to that side.

Like most other Jews on the platform that day, Frankl was not sure what had happened. Ninety percent of the people on his train had been sent to the left. That night, Frankl found out that they all were dead.

Gas Chambers and Crematoria

The Nazis built **gas chambers** especially designed to murder people. They also built several **crematoria** where they installed furnaces to burn the bodies of their victims.

Both the gas chambers and the crematoria were built by leading German companies. Although they knew exactly what they were building, the companies considered the job as a business deal. They made a profit, and those who did the work were well paid.

The people sentenced to death were taken to large rooms. They were told to remove their clothes. Even at this late stage, the Nazis tried to deceive their victims. The Nazis told the Jews that they were about to shower. Each person was given a bar of soap. There was a sign on the wall that said "to the baths." Inside the gas chambers were false shower heads.

The poison gas entered the gas chambers through vents in the floor. The gas was called **Zyklon B** and was very poisonous. There were horrible screams as people struggled to breathe. (See the Going to the Source section.)

In 15 to 20 minutes, everyone in the gas chambers was dead. Unlike the mass shootings, gassing did not force the killers to face their victims. Special teams of prisoners removed the bodies from the gas chambers and took them to the crematoria where the bodies were burned. At Auschwitz, the Nazis used these methods to murder up to 12,000 people per day.

Medical Experiments

Barbaric medical experiments were among the many horrors at Auschwitz. These experiments were conducted by SS doctors. One of the Nazis' goals was to eliminate all groups of people that they found inferior. Therefore, they experimented to find a fast way to **sterilize** these people. To sterilize people means to make them unable to have children.

Just as horrible were the experiments that Dr. Josef Mengele conducted on hundreds of sets of Jewish twins.

Vera and Olga Kriegel were twin sisters who were victims of Mengele's experiments. The girls were five years old when Mengele first experimented on them. Years later in Jerusalem, Vera summed up her experience in Auschwitz. She had thought that "perhaps I was already in Hell."

Slave Labor

The Nazis made use of slave laborers in camps all over Europe. Jews as well as non-Jews worked in these camps under horrible conditions. The Nazis used these slave laborers to support their war machine. The Nazis needed workers to replace the millions of men who were in the armed forces.

GOING TO THE SOURCE

Jews Murdered by Gassing At Auschwitz

Dr. Johann Paul Kremer kept a diary while serving as an SS doctor at Auschwitz. He was one of many German doctors who served the SS. After the war, Dr. Kremer was tried for his crimes in Poland and was sentenced to death. He was later released and returned to Germany. The excerpt below is from September 2, 1942, when Kremer took part in the gassing of Jews from France, including 148 children under the age of 15.

These mass murders took place in small cottages situated [located] outside the Birkenau camp in a wood. . . . All SS physicians on duty in the camp took turns to participate in the gassing. . . . My part as a physician at the gassing consisted in remaining in readiness near the [cottage].

I was brought there by car. I sat in front with the driver, and an SS hospital orderly sat in the back of the car with [an] oxygen apparatus to revive SS men employed in the gassing, in case any of them should succumb [fall victim] to the poisonous fumes.

When the transport with people who were destined to be gassed arrived at the railway ramp, the SS officers selected, from among the new arrivals, persons fit to work, while the rest—old people, all children, women with children in their arms and other persons not deemed fit to work—were . . . driven to the gas-chambers.

I used to follow behind the transport till we reached the bunker. There people were first driven into the barrack huts where the victims undressed and then went naked to the gas-chambers. Very often no incidents occurred, as the SS men kept people quiet, maintaining that they were to bathe and be deloused.

After driving all of them into the gas-chamber, the door was closed and an SS man in a gas-mask threw the contents of a Cyclon [Zyklon] tin through an opening in the side wall. The shouting and screaming of the victims could be heard through the opening and it was clear that they were fighting for their lives.

From Johann Paul Kremer, *Diary of Johann Paul Kremer: Auschwitz Seen Though the Eyes of the SS*. 2nd edition, edited by Kazimierz Smolen, Oswiecim, 1978.

1. What was Dr. Kremer's role in the gassing of the Jewish prisoners?
2. What happened at the "selection"?

Germany's leading companies also eagerly made use of slave labor. Among those companies were Daimler-Benz, the makers of Mercedes automobiles; BMW, another leading automobile maker; the huge steel and arms maker Krupp; and Siemens, the electrical giant.

At Auschwitz, I.G. Farben constructed a huge series of factories to make artificial rubber. The slave laborers at I.G. Farben and other projects at Auschwitz were literally worked to death. When the workers weakened from starvation or disease, the Nazis sent them to the gas chambers. While they remained alive, the workers endured vicious and cruel punishments. Meanwhile, the owners of I.G. Farben made huge profits.

It is not accurate to call these workers slaves. Slave owners usually view their slaves as their property and want to keep them alive. At Auschwitz and at other Nazi camps, the goal was to work the prisoners to death. Theodore Lehman, a survivor, explained why Jews at Auschwitz were "not slaves, but less than slaves."

The machinery had to be operated with care, oiled, greased, and allowed to rest; its life span was protected. We, on the other hand, were like a bit of sandpaper, which, rubbed a few times, becomes useless and is thrown away to be burned with the garbage.

The End of Auschwitz

In October 1944, hundreds of Jewish inmates at Auschwitz revolted. They killed several SS guards and destroyed one crematorium before the Nazis put down the revolt.

By late 1944, the Russian army was overrunning all of Poland. As the Russians neared Auschwitz, the SS evacuated some of the prisoners from Auschwitz. The SS desperately wanted to destroy the evidence of the Nazis' huge crime. Before fleeing, the SS also blew up crematoria, destroyed furnaces, and burned documents.

When the Nazis also removed the surviving Jews from the camp, they forced the Jews to

At the end of World War II, only a few of the slave laborers were alive. They gathered at the gates of Auschwitz to greet the victorious Allies. Starved and exhausted, many died shortly after they were liberated.

march west ahead of the approaching Soviet army. Thousands of Jews died from the cold or were shot during these "death marches."

On January 27, 1945, the Soviet army entered Auschwitz and found about 7,600 Jews, many near death. These survivors were all that was left of the 1.5 million human beings the Nazis had brought to Auschwitz.

Thinking It Over

1. Why did the Nazis give bars of soap to the Jews as they were led to the gas chambers at Auschwitz?
2. What was the role of I.G. Farben at Auschwitz?

Case Study Review

Identifying Main Ideas

1. What occurred at the Wannsee Conference?
2. How did the Nazis use technology to accomplish the Final Solution?
3. (a) What was the process of "selection?"
   (b) How did the Nazis select those who were fit to work?

Working Together

Based on the information in this case study, design a booklet or pamphlet to inform people about the horrors of Auschwitz. With several classmates, make a list of the topics you will cover in your booklet. You might include such topics as how Jews were transported, where victims were transported from, and the conditions in the camps. Then consider how you will organize and present the information so that people will understand it. Display your final work to your class and ask for feedback.

Active Learning

Creating a Map Review the notes that you have taken on the location of the death camps and on the places from which Jews were deported. Prepare a map that shows this information. You may use the map on page 54 as a starting point. You may wish to use your school or local library to find other maps of Europe. An excellent source is Martin Gilbert's *Atlas of the Holocaust*. Your map should indicate the countries from which Jews were deported, the routes that some of the trains took, and the locations of the Nazi death camps.

Lessons for Today

English writer Rudyard Kipling (1865–1936) wrote, "All the people like us are we, and everyone else is they." What did Kipling mean by this statement? Do you think the Nazis would have agreed with Kipling? Why or why not? Do you think that many people in the United States share Kipling's attitude? Explain.

What Might You Have Done?

Imagine that you worked for a company like Krupp or I.G. Farben during World War II. What would you have done if you found out that your employer was using slave labor or creating crematoria for the Nazi death machine? Keep in mind that your job, and perhaps your life, is at stake. Explain what your response would be.

CRITICAL THINKING
Clarifying the Issues

"I don't know what you're talking about, but I agree with it 100 percent."

"I don't understand everything you say, but I disagree with you."

Do these statements sound strange to you? Before we agree or disagree with a statement, we should be able to understand it clearly. Critical thinkers are able to identify questionable statements. We need to separate fact from opinion and to recognize a speaker's point of view.

What follows is a statement made in October 1943 by Heinrich Himmler, the head of the SS. He was speaking to the highest-ranking officers of the SS. Remember that the Nazis never mentioned the real nature of the Final Solution in public, although anyone involved in the killing knew what that term meant. In this speech, Himmler made an exception to this rule and stated directly what the Nazis meant by the Final Solution.

I want to speak to you here, in complete frankness, of a really grave matter. Amongst ourselves, for once, it shall be said quite openly, but all the same we shall never speak of it in public.... I am referring here to the evacuation of the Jews, the extermination of the Jewish people.

Most of you know what it is like to see 100 corpses side by side, or 500, or 1000. To have stood fast through this and—except for cases of human weakness—to have remained decent, that has made us hard. This is an unwritten and never-to-be-written page of glory in our history.

Himmler went on to say:

We had a moral right, we had the duty towards our people, to destroy this people that wanted to destroy us.... All in all, however, we can say that we have carried out this most difficult of tasks in a spirit of love for our people. We have suffered no harm to our inner being, our soul, our character.

Ending his speech, Himmler said:

We want to be worthy of having been permitted to be the first SS men of the Fuhrer [leader], Adolf Hitler, in the long history of the Germanic people which stretches before us. We now direct our thoughts to the Fuhrer, our Fuhrer, Adolf Hitler, who will create the Germanic Reich [empire] and will lead us into the Germanic future.

1. Himmler admitted that the extermination of the Jews was a "never-to-be-written" page in German history. Yet he also called it a "page of glory." Why do you think Himmler and the other Nazis leaders felt they had to hide something that they called a "page of glory"?

2. Himmler said that the Nazis had a "moral right" and a "duty" to exterminate the Jews because the Jews "wanted to destroy us." Did the Nazis use facts as evidence to back up the claim that the Jews wanted to destroy Germany? When you read about the Jews of Germany earlier in this book, what did you learn about their feelings about Germany?

3. It is very possible that Himmler believed most or all of what he said to his SS officers. What does that tell you about his ability to separate fact from opinion? What does that tell you about Himmler's perspective on the Holocaust?

THE YOUNGEST VICTIMS: CHILDREN OF THE HOLOCAUST

Children were the most innocent victims of the Holocaust. About 15,000 Jewish children were sent to Theresienstadt, a concentration camp. Fewer than 100 survived.

CRITICAL QUESTIONS

- What was the fate of most Jewish children during the Holocaust?
- How did a few children manage to survive?

TERMS TO KNOW

- Theresienstadt
- Aktion
- Kinderaktion
- Ponary
- partisan

ACTIVE LEARNING

After you read this case study, you will be asked to create a memorial for the children who were murdered in the Holocaust. The memorial can be a statue, plaque, or sculpture. As you read, look for the Active Learning boxes. They will suggest points at which you might want to take notes for your memorial.

Franta Bass was born in Czechoslovakia in 1930. In 1941, at the age of 11, he was deported from his home and sent to a concentration camp called **Theresienstadt.**

Before World War II, Theresienstadt was known as Terezín. It was a walled town of about 3,700 people in the mountains near the Czech capital of Prague. Once the Nazis turned Terezín into a concentration camp, they crowded over 50,000 Jews inside.

While at Theresienstadt, Franta wrote poems. One of them was called "The Garden."

> *A little garden,*
> *Fragrant and full of roses.*
> *The path is narrow*
> *And a little boy walks along it.*
>
> *A little boy, a sweet boy,*
> *Like that growing blossom.*
> *When that blossom comes to bloom,*
> *The little boy will be no more.*

Franta was thinking about his own future when he wrote this poem. Tragically, the poem accurately predicted his fate. In 1944, Franta was sent from Theresienstadt to Auschwitz. There he was murdered in the gas chambers. He was 14 years old.

Between 1941 and 1944, the Nazis imprisoned 15,000 Jewish children under the age of 15 at Theresienstadt. Less than 100 of the 15,000 survived the Holocaust. The 15,000 children from Theresienstadt represented only a fraction of the 1.2 million Jewish children the Nazis murdered in the Holocaust.

Franta Bass and the other children of Theresienstadt wrote many poems and made over 5,000 drawings and collages. Through art and poetry the children expressed their fears and sometimes their hopes. Some of their poems tell about their powerful will to live. Others, such as Franta Bass's poem entitled "I am a Jew," described their pride as Jews.

> *I am a Jew and will be a Jew forever.*
> *Even if I should die from hunger,*
> *never will I submit.*
> *I will always fight for my people,*
> *on my honor.*
> *I will never be ashamed of them,*
> *I give my word.*
>
> *I am proud of my people,*
> *how dignified they are.*
> *Even though I am suppressed,*
> *I will always come back to life.*

A Good Book to Read

...I never saw another butterfly...Children's Drawings and Poems from Terezín Concentration Camp, 1942–1944, expanded 2nd edition, edited by Hana Volavkova, Schocken Books, New York, 1993.

The Nazis used Terezín (Theresienstadt) as a "model" to cover up their crimes and allowed the Red Cross to visit it. The 15,000 children imprisoned there were given materials so that they could write and draw. The pictures and poems collected in this volume tell how the children suffered and struggled to keep their hopes alive.

1 The Nazi War on Jewish Children

The systematic killing of children was perhaps the most horrible of all the Nazis' crimes. At the trial of Nazi war criminal Adolf Eichmann in 1961, Gideon Hausner, Israel's Attorney General, said:

> *No part of all [the] bloody work is so shocking and terrible as that of the million Jewish children whose blood was spilled like water throughout Europe.*

GOING TO THE SOURCE

Poetry from Terezín

Even in their darkest hour, the children of Terezín created poetry and drawings that expressed their love of life and their will to survive. Below is a poem written by a young child of Terezín.

The Butterfly
The last, the very last,
So richly, brightly, dazzlingly yellow.
Perhaps if the sun's tears would sing
   against a white stone. . . .

Such, such a yellow
Is carried lightly 'way up high.
It went away I'm sure because it wished to
   kiss the world good-bye.

For seven weeks I've lived in here,
Penned up inside this ghetto.
But I have found what I love here.
The dandelions call to me
And the white chestnut branches in the court.
Only I never saw another butterfly.

That butterfly was the last one.
Butterflies don't live in here,
   in the ghetto.

Pavel Friedmann

From . . . *I never saw another butterfly . . .Children's Drawings and Poems from Terezín Concentration Camp*, 1942–1944, edited by Hana Volavkova, New York: Schocken Books, 1993, pp. 39 and 55.

1. What did Pavel Friedmann find to love in the ghetto?
2. The mood of a poem is the feeling it creates in the reader. How would you describe the mood of "The Butterfly"?

Hausner went on to describe children who were murdered in front of their parents. He told of children who were forced to watch their parents beaten or murdered. He described children in ghettos who came home to find their parents already sent off to death camps. He mentioned children who each day lived in terror that their hiding places would be discovered. He spoke of children driven to open mass graves and shot. He described children who were starved, gassed, or worked to death.

Hausner explained that it was the Nazis' intention to wipe out the Jewish people. The murder of Jewish children was, therefore, a central goal of the Holocaust. Nothing was allowed to stand in the way of that goal.

"Sir, I Would Like To Live..."

The Nazis believed that Jewish children were a threat to the German people. An SS officer explained why at his trial. He said the killing of the young was necessary because "the children were people who would grow up." When they were grown they would become a danger "no smaller than that of their parents."

The Einsatzgruppen were the special SS units assigned to kill Jews. At times, they were devoted strictly to killing Jewish children. One SS officer described how he and his fellow Nazis killed a group of children between the ages of six and twelve.

> *I drove the children to the brink of a ditch where another SS man stood. . . . He shot them with his submachine gun and then . . . kicked them into the ditch. The children knew what to expect and attempted to run away. They beseeched the executioners: "Sir, I am scared! Sir, I would like to live, don't shoot me."*

Active Learning: Make notes on what Gideon Hausner said about the Nazis' intention. Also be sure to remember incidents such as the one described above when you plan your memorial.

Kinderaktion

The SS did not stop with murdering Jewish children. It did everything it could to prevent Jewish children from being born. A pregnant woman in a concentration camp faced the death

About 1.2 million Jewish children were killed in the Holocaust. According to the Nazis, Jewish children were a threat to the German people. Here, Jewish children arrive at Auschwitz-Birkenau.

penalty. In one ghetto in Lithuania, the SS pronounced the death penalty on the infant, the mother, and the *whole family*.

All across Europe, the SS conducted raids called **Aktions.** Aktions were general roundups of Jews. Raids to round up pregnant women and young children were called **Kinderaktions**. No place was safe, not even isolated villages.

On April 6, 1944, German forces moved into a small mountain village in France. There, over 40 Jewish children lived in a children's home. The Nazis rounded them up and threw them into transports "like packages." They sent all of these children to their deaths at Auschwitz.

Children in Hiding

Some children found hiding places among the non-Jewish population in Europe. These children lived in permanent fear of the SS and local police. From France in the west to the Ukraine in the east, local police often helped the SS find Jews in hiding.

Even very young children were aware of the dangers that discovery would bring. When Daisy Miller was five years old, she hid with her family in a farm house. Once a stranger saw her. She felt that she wanted to "fall through the floor and disappear, I just wanted to melt away into nothing." Although only five, Daisy knew that discovery "meant the worst of everything."

Children even younger than Daisy Miller understood the danger of being discovered. Adults were amazed that children three or four years old understood so much. They "clammed up when it was necessary, they knew when to hide." When one small child was offered a pill to calm him, he told the doctor, "This is not necessary, I shall be quiet, I shall not scream."

Children in the Ghettos

Children inside the ghettos had to worry about being hunted down during Kinderaktions and deported to death camps. However, even when they were not being deported, they died by the tens of thousands. Hunger, cold, and disease killed them.

Jewish communities in the ghettos did what they could to help children. But the needs of the children were too great and the resources to small. Each day more children became orphans when their parents died or were deported. The Judenrat of the Warsaw Ghetto declared a "Children's Month" to help its 100,000 children. It put up posters that said "Our children must not die" and "Our children are sacred." But there was not enough food, clothing, or shelter to care for many of the children of Warsaw.

Mary Berg was 16 years old when she lived in the Warsaw Ghetto. In her diary, she wrote about the "great number" of children "whose parents have died, and who sit in rags on the streets." Many of them were so starved that they "no longer have a human appearance." Mary wrote how many of the children she saw "no longer beg for bread, but for death."

Hunger ruled the lives of children in the ghetto. Even those who were stronger and were better off knew they had little chance of survival. They faced death as bravely as they could in a world that had robbed them of their childhood.

Thinking It Over

1. What was the Kinderaktion?
2. Why did the Nazis consider Jewish children a danger?

2 A Child in the Vilna Ghetto

Yitzhak Rudashevski was born in 1927 in the city of Vilna. For centuries, Vilna was a major

Jewish cultural center. Before World War II, the city was part of Poland. Today it is called Vilnius and is the capital of Lithuania.

Yitzhak was an only child. His father was a typesetter for a Yiddish newspaper. His mother worked as a seamstress. Yitzhak was an excellent student. His special interest was history. Yitzhak also took an active part in Jewish youth activities.

June 24, 1941, marked the end of life as Yitzhak knew it. That was the day the German army took over Vilna. At the time, about 60,000 Jews lived there. Few would remain living at the end of the war.

Yitzhak kept a diary of his life in Vilna between June 1941 and April 1943. It tells how this teenage boy tried to stay alive both physically and mentally in a world dominated by death.

The Nazis in Vilna

The Nazis brought death and terror to Vilna even before they set up the ghettos. In the summer of 1941, Yitzhak told how the Jews in one neighborhood had been led out. But, he remarked, "we do not know where."

Yitzhak later found out that the people were taken to a killing ground in the woods outside Vilna called **Ponary.** There the people were shot and buried in mass graves. The Nazis murdered over 30,000 Jews at Ponary during the second half of 1941.

The Jews left behind in Vilna also suffered. As Yitzhak wrote:

> It is the night between the fifth and sixth of September, a beautiful, sleepless September night, people like shadows.

Young people in the ghettos did what they could to survive. These young men are attempting to buy food from people outside the ghetto. All knew that the penalty for smuggling food into the ghetto was death.

People sit in helpless, painful expectation with their bundles. Tomorrow we shall be led to the ghetto.

Yitzhak realized that life would never be the same again for himself and his fellow Jews.

Here is the ghetto gate. I feel that I have been robbed, my freedom is being robbed from me, my home, and the familiar Vilna streets I love so much.

Inside the ghetto Yitzhak, his parents, and his grandmother shared one room with eleven other people. The first night in the ghetto Yitzhak could not sleep. He listened all night to the "restless breathing of people with whom I have been suddenly thrown together, people who just like me have suddenly been uprooted from their homes."

Forced into Hiding

Soon people were pulled out of the ghetto. Jews with special skills or certain jobs were given yellow work permits. Others were deported to Ponary.

Yitzhak's parents did not have the special work permits. The family knew it was doomed. They went into hiding.

Yitzhak's family joined other Jews in a warehouse that had a secret entrance. The Germans sent Lithuanian police to find the Jews. Yitzhak described the scene.

The hide-out is becoming fuller and fuller. We are finally so crowded together we cannot move....We are like animals surrounded by the hunter. The hunter is on all sides; beneath us, above us, from the sides. I feel the enemy under the boards on which I am standing.... They pound, tear, break....Suddenly ...a child bursts into tears....We are lost....A desperate attempt to shove sugar into the child's mouth is of no avail. They stop up the child's mouth with pillows. The mother of the child is weeping.

Somehow the police did not hear the crying child and the group was not discovered. Yitzhak

wrote how "my heart beat with such joy. I have remained alive." The ordeal had lasted six hours. Shortly after this event, Yitzhak's mother managed to get a yellow work permit that "grants the right to life."

"Today We Go To School."

As in other Jewish ghettos, the Jews in the Vilna ghetto set up schools for their children. Going to school gave children much more than an education. It gave them hope for the future.

Yitzhak was overjoyed when he returned to school in October 1942. "Finally I have lived to see the day. Today we go to school." The other children felt the same way. "There is a happy spirit in the school," Yitzhak wrote.

Jewish children, like these from the city of Lodz in Poland, were rounded up and sent to the death camps. Jewish children were forced to watch their parents beaten or shot. Many were taken to open mass graves and shot. Others were starved to death. Most were sent to the gas chambers of the death camps.

Yitzhak was proud when he earned good grades, even though he admitted that they "could have been better." He and his classmates managed to remain hopeful. In January 1943, Yitzhak wrote:

Our spirit, which we bear proudly within the ghetto walls, will be the most beautiful gift to the newly rising future. Long live youth!— the progress of our people.

By the beginning of 1943, Yitzhak had a real reason for hope. The Germans were being defeated on the battlefield! Yitzhak knew that the Americans and British had beaten the Germans in North Africa. He learned of the great Soviet victory in the city of Stalingrad, over 1,000 miles east of Vilna. "The people in the ghetto are celebrating.... At last the Germans have suffered a gigantic defeat."

Active Learning: When you think about the Jewish children murdered in the Holocaust, remember their bravery. Keep track of what Yitzhak did to keep his spirits up under the worst of conditions.

Emptying the Ghettos

Unfortunately, these defeats that the Germans suffered would not save Yitzhak and the remaining Jews of Vilna. In the spring of 1943, the Germans started emptying the ghettos around Vilna. In Vilna the people were

Some Jewish children survived because of the bravery of others. Eve Nisencqajg (fifth from left) was born in 1936 in Poland. During the war, she was placed in hiding with a Polish Catholic couple. Eve posed as their niece, and is shown here during a first communion ceremony. Eve survived the war and in 1947, emigrated to Canada.

"depressed and mournful. We are unprotected and exposed to death."

Yitzhak's last entry in his diary is dated April 1943. His family then went into hiding. In October, the Germans found them and murdered them at Ponary.

One of Yitzhak's cousins managed to escape the Germans. She joined a group of **partisans.** The partisans were small bands of civilians who hid in the woods and fought the Germans. After the war, she returned to the family hiding place and found Yitzhak's diary. It was published in Israel in 1968.

Thinking It Over

1. Why were the yellow work permits so important?
2. Why was Yitzhak happy to go to school?

3 Children in Hiding

It was 1946—about a year after the end of World War II. A Jewish official arrived in Poland. He was looking for Jewish children who had survived the Holocaust. At first, he found none. Then slowly children began to come out of their hiding places.

Some had been hidden by non-Jewish families during the war. Others were taken into monasteries or convents. Some were baptized and were forbidden to return to their original Jewish identities after the war. Others were not allowed to forget that they were really Jews pretending to be Christians.

Some children managed to survive in the forests. A few more managed to find shelter in isolated villages.

The official eventually found more than 1,000 children. Throughout Europe there were thousands more. Some had survived with their parents, others with brothers or sisters. There were children who had joined partisan bands. Miraculously, a few children somehow made it through the war alone.

Jewish children in hiding lived in attics and in cellars. They hid in caves and lived in barns with animals.

Some children lived openly with non-Jewish families. Often their parents had managed to get them false identity papers so they could pretend to be non-Jews. Sometimes their non-Jewish families were paid to take them in. At

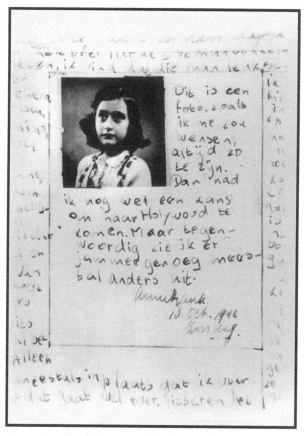

Anne Frank left Germany for the Netherlands with her family to escape the Nazis. In 1942, as a 13-year-old, she went into hiding in an abandoned office. She was discovered in 1945, and sent off to a concentration camp where she died at the age of 16. Her diary describes her life in hiding.

other times, non-Jews volunteered to care for Jewish children at great risk to themselves.

"You Are No Longer Jana Levi"

In the summer of 1942, eight-year-old Jana Levi and her cousin were secretly taken from the ghetto in the Polish city of Cracow. Jana's father paid thousands of dollars for the two children to be brought to a farm where they could live with a Polish family.

The children's cover story was that they were Polish children whose parents had disappeared. They had forged identification papers to back up their story.

On the journey to the farm, Jana was told, "You are no longer Jana Levi; forget the name. You were not born in Cracow." She was told who her Polish parents were, where she was born, her new birthday, and other information. The eight-year-old also was warned, "Make sure you don't speak about your home. Make sure you don't talk." Jana's father had expected that the Polish family would treat his child well and educate her. Instead, Jana had to work hard all day. She did everything from cleaning the stables and working in the fields to baking bread and cleaning floors.

Although she was safer than most Jewish children, Jana had to be very careful not to give herself away. One false step or one careless word could have meant being caught.

Kept Indoors

Jewish children in hiding often had to stay indoors for months and even years at a time. Some children hid in very small spaces. These spaces were so small that most people could not have withstood them for even a short time.

Gabrielle Siltern was not yet ten years old when she hid from the Germans in attics. There were no toys, so she and her friends invented a game.

In the spaces between these beams [in the attics] live rats with their families. We would walk on the beams to get to the spaces where the rat families lived and then poke at them with a stick and watch them jump.

Other children were even more restricted. Ephraim Shtenkler's parents paid a non-Jewish family to hide him. For several years, the family kept him in a cupboard and under a bed. As a result, at the age of six Ephraim could not walk.

After the war, Ephraim told of his suffering. He told how he learned that his father had been captured and killed. He also told of watching other children playing outside. "I wanted to cry," he said. "It was already three to four years and I hadn't gone out of doors."

Jana, Gabrielle, and Ephraim were the lucky ones. They survived. Most of the Jewish children who tried to hide from the Nazis were caught and murdered.

Thinking It Over

1. Why was Jana Levi told to forget her name?
2. Why was Ephraim Shtenkler unable to walk?

Case Study Review

Identifying Main Ideas

1. Reread Franta Bass's poems on page 66. What were the messages of the two poems?
2. What was Ponary? What happened to Jews who were sent to Ponary?
3. How did non-Jews sometimes help Jewish children survive?

Working Together

Form a small group. Your assignment is to write a dialogue among the members of a Jewish family that has decided to send one of its children to live with a non-Jewish family. First, decide which family members will be featured in your dialogue. Then, brainstorm to create the details of the situation. Details might include where the family is from and how the family found a non-Jewish family willing to take the child. Next, write a first draft of your dialogue. Work as a group to revise your draft. Read your final version to the rest of the class.

 ## Active Learning

Creating a Memorial Review the notes you took as you read this case study. Decide what you want the focus of your memorial to be. For example, it might focus on how the Nazis treated the children, or it might focus on what the children did to save themselves. Next, decide on the form that your memorial will take. Sketch your ideas on a sheet of paper. If possible, create a three-dimensional model of your memorial to display in class.

Lessons for Today

Jewish children who grew up during the Holocaust had to develop new skills very quickly in order to survive. Jana Levi was only eight when she had to leave her family and learn a new way of life. At the age of 14, Yitzhak Rudashevski had to adjust to terrible conditions in a ghetto and somehow keep his mind on a better future.

While we do not face the terror of the Holocaust, some children must suddenly adjust to new and difficult conditions in their lives. How can we learn to cope when bad things happen?

What Might You Have Done?

Imagine that you are hiding with a crowd of other people in a warehouse. Suddenly, the police burst in and begin to search the warehouse. What would you try to think about in order to control your fear? Explain your answer.

CRITICAL THINKING
Exploring the Consequences

Consequences

A consequence is something that happens as a result of an action. Short-term consequences follow soon after the action. Long-term consequences follow later. Consequences themselves often lead to other consequences.

Actions have consequences. Some consequences happen immediately after an action. For example, if you do not study for an exam, the immediate consequence is a poor grade. Other consequences occur over a longer period of time. For example, if you do poorly in school, you may not get into college.

You already know of the many horrible immediate consequences of the Holocaust. However, the long-term consequences are also important. The 1.5 million children who died in the Holocaust never had the chance to become adults, to have children of their own, and to use their talents and abilities. There also were painful consequences for the Jewish children who survived the Holocaust. Many were orphans who lost their entire families. Many were physically or emotionally scarred.

Copy the diagram below in your notebook. Use it to consider both long-term and short-term consequences of the Holocaust. Use the questions below to help you fill in the diagram.

1. What were the short-term effects of the Holocaust on children who were forced to live in ghettos or who went into hiding?

2. What do you think were some the long-term effects for children who survived the Holocaust?

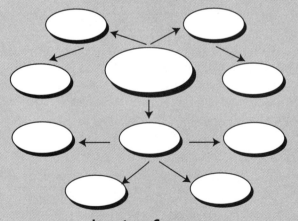

Short-term Consequences

Long-term Consequences

Danish fishermen ferry a boatload of Jewish refugees across the sea to neutral Sweden. Within a few days of the first arrests by Germans in 1943, about 70,000 Danish Jews escaped the country.

NON-JEWS WHO HELPED JEWS

CRITICAL QUESTIONS

■ What motivated non-Jews to risk their own lives to help Jews during the Holocaust?

■ How were non-Jews honored for their courageous acts during the Holocaust?

TERMS TO KNOW

■ collaborator
■ Huguenot
■ diplomat
■ Arrow Cross

ACTIVE LEARNING

This case study contains several stories about non-Jews who helped Jews during the Holocaust. Imagine that you have been asked to create a script for a television series about these acts of bravery and kindness. As you read this case study, try to imagine what the people in the stories were thinking and feeling. Take notes about the stories that will help you create your script.

It was a cold and rainy night in October 1942. Two Jewish children stood in the train station of Piotrkow, Poland. They mixed with passengers who had just gotten off a train. They hoped nobody would notice them.

Ruska Gutterman was 18. Her younger brother Benek was 16. They had just fled from the local ghetto. The Jews of the ghetto were about to be deported to the Treblinka death camp.

The Gutterman children had false identity papers. Unlike many Polish Jews, they spoke Polish without a Yiddish accent. They both knew something about the Catholic religion. Neither child had the dark hair or skin tone common among Jews in Eastern Europe.

In short, Ruska and Benek looked and could act like Catholic Poles. That was why their parents sent them from the ghetto. The parents had stayed behind to face deportation with their youngest child.

But now, Ruska and Benek were in trouble. Their train out of Piotrkow had been canceled. It was about 10 P.M. and there would not be another train until 4 A.M. Soon the train station would be empty. If Ruska and Benek did not find a hiding place, the Germans would catch them. Then they would be doomed.

Ruska was desperate. Then she noticed a railway worker leaving the station. Ruska thought that "he had a kind face." She took a chance and walked up to him. Ruska said she and Benek needed a place to spend the night since their train was not leaving till 4 A.M. It was against the law to be on the street.

The man took the children to his apartment. Ruska heard his wife and a baby in the next room. The wife asked, "Jan, what's going on." He answered, "It's nothing. . . . Go back to sleep."

Jan told Ruska and Benek to go to sleep. He would wake them in time for their train. "He knows we're Jewish," Ruska thought. She was sure Jan would turn them in to the police.

Just before 4 A.M. Jan returned. He took the children down to the street himself. Ruska noticed his trembling hands. Then Jan said, "My God. What they're doing to your people. . . . I can't take it."

Ruska was right. Jan did know that she and Benek were Jewish. But he was risking his life to help them. "God be with you," he said.

Ruska thanked Jan and offered him money for his help. He answered firmly, "No, you keep it. You're going to need it a lot more than I will." Ruska later remembered:

> I reached for his hand and kissed it, for there was no other way of expressing the great flood of gratitude I felt. In a world of enemies, this man—a total stranger—had given us our lives.

Ruska and Benek were among the few lucky ones. They escaped death that day and survived the war because a man named Jan did what he knew was right.

World War II began with the lightning-fast invasion of Poland by German troops.

1 Who Helped the Jews?

What did non-Jews in Nazi-controlled areas do to help the Jews? There is no single answer to that question. People behaved differently from country to country and from town to town. Even within a single family, some members tried to help the Jews while others turned them over to the Nazis.

Many people actually helped the Nazis. There were, however, tiny islands of support for Jews in every country. These people risked their lives to help the Jews. Because of them, tens of thousands of Jews survived the Holocaust.

Helping the Nazis

The Nazis found helpers almost everywhere in Europe. In many places, centuries of anti-Semitism meant that millions of people were prejudiced against Jews. The Nazis took advantage of that prejudice whenever they could. They also used anti-Semitic propaganda to increase hatred toward Jews.

Anti-Semitism was very strong in Poland and in Ukraine. Polish police helped the SS guard the Warsaw Ghetto. One resident of the ghetto, Emmanual Ringelblum, wrote that when Jews tried to escape, local peasants "capture them and hand them over to the Germans."

In Latvia, Lithuania, and Ukraine local police helped the Nazis round up Jews. The police also guarded the ghettos, concentration camps, and death camps. At the Babi Yar massacre, Jews were driven to the killing ground between two lines of Ukrainian police.

The Nazis also found **collaborators** in other countries across Europe. A collaborator is someone who cooperates with the enemy. In France, government officials and police helped the Nazis find Jews. Because of French collaboration, the Nazis were able to send over 76,000 Jews from France to the death camps.

The largest roundup occurred on July 16, 1942. French officials herded nearly 13,000

Senpo Sugihara was a Japanese diplomat during World War II. Although Japan and Nazi Germany were allies, Sugihara defied the Germans to help Jews escape Nazi-controlled Europe. Years after his death, he was honored by students of the Mirrer Yeshiva in Brooklyn, New York. A member of the Japanese Consulate accepted the award.

Jews into a sports arena. They included 4,000 infants, toddlers, and older children. The French officials carried and dragged the children into freight cars. Not one of them survived.

"I Felt I Had To Do Something."

It took great courage to save Jews in Nazi-controlled Europe. The Nazis did everything they could to prevent people from helping Jews. People who hid Jews were often shot or sent to concentration camps themselves. A person who did not report someone else for hiding a Jew faced the same penalties. Sometimes the Nazis punished an entire family when one of its members helped a Jew. These measures, however, did not stop everyone.

The people who helped Jews had many different reasons for their actions. Some did it for religious reasons. Eduard Fajks of Poland said he acted because:

God gives us life as [a] precious loan. No one but God has a right to reclaim it. That's all I know. The rest is unimportant.

Imre Bathory of Hungary heeded one of the first lessons in the Bible.

I know that when I stand before God on the Judgment Day, I shall not be asked the question put to Cain—where were you when your brother's blood was crying out to God?

Other people considered it their duty as human beings to help Jews. Frederick Kabbes of the Netherlands said:

It's like seeing someone drowning. You either stand on the side and don't do anything or you jump in and help. . . . It was something that had to be done.

There were people who said that helping Jews escape the Nazis was the natural thing to do. Others said they would have been too ashamed not to help. Ona Simaite of Lithuania saw what was happening to the Jews in Vilna. She "could not eat. I was ashamed not to be Jewish. I felt I had to do something." Dr. Giobanni Pesante told a Jew whom he was hiding that, "I

ask you to remain for my sake, not yours. If you leave, I shall forever be ashamed to be a member of the human race."

Thinking It Over

1. What is a collaborator?
2. How did the Nazis try to prevent people from helping Jews?

2 Rescue By Land and By Sea

Le Chambon-sur-Lignon is a small village in the mountains of southern France. Most of the people of the village are **Huguenots**, or French Protestants. The Huguenots had long been a minority in France, which is mainly Catholic. As a result, they often were the victims of persecution themselves. Perhaps their own persecution explains why the Huguenots in this small village could not turn away the Jews who came to them for help.

Shelter in Southern France

The religious leader of Le Chambon was Pastor Andre Trocme. He and his wife, Magda, organized a network to hide Jews and to get them out of France. The effort began the day Magda Trocme heard a knock on the door.

A woman knocked on my door one evening and she said she was a German Jew coming from Northern France, and that she was in danger. She heard that in Le Chambon somebody could help her. Could she come into my house? I said, "Naturally, come in, come in."

Soon there was a network that stretched throughout the region. People in Le Chambon

GOING TO THE SOURCE

A Jewish Child Survives in a Christian World

Goldie Szachter was lucky to be hidden on the farm of a Christian Polish family named Surowjecka. Because she was blond, Goldie was able to "pass" for Polish and live openly on the farm. Jewish children had to be hidden not only from the Nazis, but from Polish neighbors who often turned them in to the Germans. That is why the events that Szachter describes below took place.

A friendly merchant was passing by one day on horseback. When he saw me, he stopped. "Good morning," he greeted Mme. [Madame] Surowjecka. Then he added, "I am simply curious. Tell me, who is that child who seems to look so different?

She spontaneously responded, "Oh, she is my niece from Krakow."

"I see," responded the merchant, but he seemed to be examining me from head to toe with an intent gaze. Then, with a gentlemanly "Good day," he rode off.

Mme. Surowjecka realized she must act quickly to minimize as much as possible the differences . . . between me and the native, village peasant girls. She . . . lengthen[ed] my dresses to make them closer in style to those worn by Polish girls. For the same reason, she also combed out and stretched my curly blond hair until it was long and straight.

Gradually, Mme. Surowjecka taught me the prayers and rituals of the village church service. She showed me how Christians brought their hands together in prayer, and the proper movements they made when they crossed themselves. Soon she began taking me to church with her.

The average Pole [supported the Nazis'] treatment of Polish Jews. On one occasion, for instance, a villager commented to Mme. Surowjecka, "The Germans are really taking care of the Jews, aren't they. We're almost rid of all of them."

Mme. Surowjecka quickly countered, "Don't leap so for joy. In the meantime, you haven't survived yet yourself. The Jews are their breakfast; they have us in mind for supper."

From Goldie Szachter Kalib, *The Last Selection:
A Child's Journey Through the Holocaust.*
Amherst: University of Massachusetts Press, 1991, pp. 161–162.

1. Why did the comments of the merchant worry Madame Surowjecka?

2. What did Madame Surowjecka mean when she said, "The Jews are their breakfast, they have us in mind for supper"?

and other villages hid people in their homes. Pastor Trocme appealed to Catholics and Protestants to help. Catholic convents and monasteries also gave shelter to Jews.

Jewish children were hidden in children's homes in the region. One of the homes was run by Daniel Trocme, a cousin of the pastor. In June 1943, the Gestapo arrested Daniel. When asked to explain why he took care of Jewish children, he answered, "I defend the weak." The Gestapo sent Daniel to the Buchenwald concentration camp where he died in April 1944.

Most of the Jews did not stay in hiding. That was too dangerous. The aim was to get them to Switzerland or Spain. Most Jews went to Switzerland, since Le Chambon was closer to that country. Guides took the Jews on the dangerous journey and smuggled them across the border.

The people of Le Chambon saved over 5,000 Jewish men, women, and children. Years later, they were asked about their heroism. One of them said:

> Things had to be done, that's all, and we happened to be there to do them. Helping these people was the most natural thing in the world.

Safety in the Netherlands

Far to the north in Holland another small town saved hundreds of Jews. The town was Nieuwlande. Like the people of Le Chambon, the inhabitants of Nieuwlande were a religious minority in their country. Most Dutch people belong to the Dutch Reformed Church. The people of Nieuwlande belong to the Christian Reformed Church.

The effort in Nieuwlande was organized by Arnold Douwes. He was the son of a pastor. Over 100 people from Nieuwlande took part in Douwes's network. They saved about 500 Jews, including 100 children.

Pastor André Trocmé, at back, center, organized a network to hide Jews and get them out of France. With others in Le Chambon, France, Trocmé helped save more than 5,000 Jewish men, women, and children.

The Jews of Denmark

The most fortunate Jewish community in Nazi-controlled Europe was in Denmark. In October 1943, most Danish Jews escaped the Nazis by sea. They sailed across a narrow strait to Sweden.

Although the Germans took over Denmark in 1940, they allowed the Danes to govern themselves. Denmark was a democracy that treated all its citizens equally. Denmark's 8,000 Jews therefore felt safe.

Everything changed in 1943. In August, the Nazis ended Danish self-government. They set up direct military rule. In September, the Germans made secret plans to deport Denmark's Jews. The Jews were to be rounded up on the night of October 1. The Germans planned the deportation to take place on Rosh Hashana, the Jewish New Year. During the holiday, most Jews would be in synagogues or at home. The Nazis thought it would be easier to round them up.

On September 28, a German shipping expert in Denmark named Georg D. Duckwitz warned a Danish political leader about the Nazis' plans. Within a day, the Danish underground and the Jews received the news.

Meanwhile, a plan was already under way to save the Jews. Danes from all walks of life joined in the effort. Doctors, nurses, taxi drivers, fishermen, and government officials all played a part. First, Jews were taken from their homes and hidden in the countryside. Then they were moved in small groups to the Danish coast opposite Sweden.

Denmark's king publicly supported his country's Jews. A leading clergyman told his people:

> We shall fight for the cause that our Jewish brothers and sisters may preserve the same freedom which we ourselves value higher than life....We must obey God before we obey man.

When the Germans came for the Jews late on October 1, almost all of them already were in hiding. Over the next two weeks, small fishing boats ferried over 90 percent of Denmark's Jews to Sweden. Over 7,200 Jews were saved.

The Germans managed to catch 477 Jews. They were sent to Theresienstadt. However, the Danish government continually asked the Germans about their condition and sent them food packages. As a result, over 400 of the deported Danish Jews survived the war.

At home, the Danish people protected Jewish property. They looked after Jewish homes and businesses. Danish Christians took Jewish religious objects and guarded them in their own churches until after the war. Years later, the state of Israel honored Georg F. Duckwitz for helping to save Danish Jews during the Holocaust. Israel also honored the entire Danish people.

Active Learning: You may choose to include one of the stories in this section in your script. Think about how you would portray some of the more dramatic scenes in these episodes.

Thinking It Over

1. What was the main goal of the rescue network of Le Chambon?
2. Why were Danish Jews suddenly in danger in September 1943?

3 The Diplomat and the Thief

Individuals also helped save Jews. Raoul Wallenberg was one of these individuals. Another was Leopold Socha. In this section, you will read about Wallenberg and Socha.

Wallenberg: The Diplomat

Wallenberg came from a wealthy Swedish banking family. Sweden was one of the few European countries that was neutral during World War II. In the spring of 1944, the Swedish government sent Raoul Wallenberg as a **diplomat** to Hungary. A diplomat represents his or her country in dealings with other countries.

Wallenberg's mission was to help the Jews of Hungary. His mission would not be easy. Hungary was an ally of Nazi Germany.

Raoul Wallenberg, who came from a wealthy Swedish banking family, risked his life to help the Jews of Hungary. He worked day and night to get Jews passports and other papers that would put them under Swedish protection. He also stood up to the German SS when they started sending Jews on death marches to the concentration camps.

A Good Movie to See

Raoul Wallenberg: Between the Lines, directed by Karin Altmann, Rhino Home Video, Santa Monica, California, 1991.

Raoul Wallenberg stood up against the Nazis' ruthless campaign to exterminate the Jews of Hungary. Following the war, Wallenberg was imprisoned as a spy in the Soviet Union. He was never heard from again. This film combines interviews, newsreels, and rare footage to tell the story of Wallenberg's personal courage and heroic efforts.

Wallenberg reached Budapest, Hungary's capital, in July. In March, Germany had sent soldiers to occupy Hungary. Between March and July, the Hungarian government deported over 400,000 Jews to Auschwitz. The deportations stopped just as Wallenberg arrived. He immediately began to help Jews receive food and medical care. He also gave out passports and other papers to put them under Swedish protection.

Then with the help of the Nazis, a group called the **Arrow Cross** seized power in Hungary. The Arrow Cross was the Hungarian version of the German Nazi party. It immediately began deporting Hungary's remaining Jews as quickly as it could. Those deported included Jews supposedly under Wallenberg's protection.

Wallenberg began to work day and night. He continued to issue thousands of Swedish passports and other Swedish documents. He used bribes and threats to get Hungarian officials to recognize the documents. Wallenberg also stood up to German SS officers in order to protect Jews.

In November 1944, the SS began its "death marches" to move Jews out of Hungary. Wallenberg caught up with the marches and saved as many Jews as he could. Seventeen-year-old Miriam Herzog was one of them.

Jewish women and girls were being forced to walk "20 or 30 miles a day in the freezing rain." Suddenly Miriam was aware of great excitement. "It's Wallenberg," the women shouted. That day, he managed to save 100 people.

When the Soviet army entered Budapest, about 100,000 Hungarian Jews were still alive. Wallenberg and other diplomats working with him deserve the credit for saving most of them.

However, Wallenberg's story has a tragic ending. For unknown reasons the Soviets arrested him. He was never seen again. The Soviet government refused to tell Wallenberg's family or the Swedish government exactly what happened to him. To this day his fate remains a mystery.

Socha: The Thief

Leopold Socha could not have been more different from Raoul Wallenberg. Socha was a Catholic who lived in Lvov, Poland. He had a job as a sewer worker. Socha used his knowledge of the sewers to carry on another job. He also was a professional thief. The sewers were an excellent place to hide his stolen goods.

In June 1943, the Nazis were deporting the last remaining Jews of the Lvov ghetto to Treblinka. The Gestapo had the ghetto surrounded. There was no way out. Among the desperate Jews looking for a hiding place was Halina Wind.

We did not know what to do. We went down with a group into the basement through a pipe,

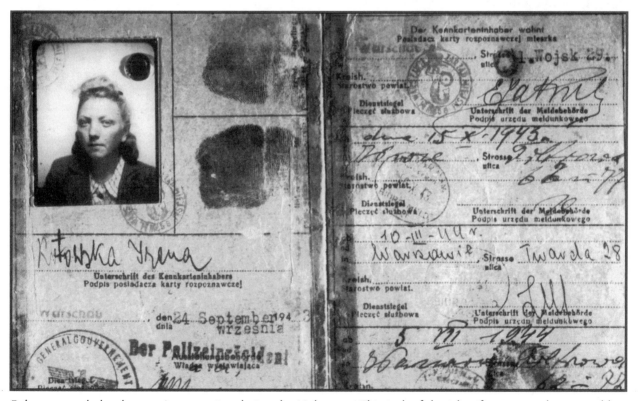

False papers helped many Jews survive during the Holocaust. This is the false identification card, stamped by the Nazi rulers of Warsaw, of Rose Stein-Braseliten. She survived by hiding outside the Warsaw Ghetto and by using the name Irena Kotosawa.

steps, water, a tunnel, other pipes. Finally we were crawling in the sewers of Lvov.

Halina's group found itself on a narrow ledge. In front of them was a river. Other groups of Jews were in the sewers. Whenever Halina heard a splash, she knew someone fell into the river and drowned.

Then Halina saw Leopold Socha. He took her and 20 other Jews to a safer place in the sewer. "Don't budge from here," he told them. "Just trust me."

Socha returned the next day. He brought food and terrible news. "The ghetto is burning," he said, "Now only you are left." Most of the other Jews in the sewers had drowned and their bodies were in the river.

Socha returned with food every day that followed. Some of the food he had stolen. Some he had bought with money Halina and her group gave him. Once a week, he took dirty clothing from them, which his wife Magdalene washed and ironed. Socha also brought the group books to read.

Soon, however, their money ran out. When the Jews offered to leave, Socha told them that they must stay.

Either you all survive or nobody. As long as you are my responsibility you are all equal to me.

Socha was a religious man. He was a Catholic who respected the Jewish religion. He brought his group a prayer book and candles for the Jewish Sabbath.

A year later, ten members of the group were still alive. Then on July 17, 1944, he shouted down to them, "Get ready, you are free." The

Active Learning: If you choose to write about Socha's life in your script, compare his attitude toward the people he was hiding to that of some of the other people you have read about.

Soviet army had driven the Germans from Lvov. Socha took the little group to his home where he and Magdalene celebrated with them.

Like Wallenberg's, Socha's story also ended tragically. Several months later, he was hit by a truck. Halina remembered that as Socha lay dying "with the blood dripping into the sewers," his anti-Semitic neighbors said that God was punishing him "for hiding Jews."

Today the state of Israel honors Leopold Socha as one of the "Righteous Among the Nations." They are the heroic non-Jews who risked their lives to save Jews during the Holocaust.

Thinking It Over

1. How did Wallenberg work to save the Jews of Hungary?
2. What did Leopold Socha tell the Jews in the sewer when they ran out of money?

Case Study Review

Identifying Main Ideas

1. What were some of the reasons non-Jews risked their lives to help Jews escape from the Nazis?

2. What did the people of Le Chambon and Nieuwlande have in common that might have led them to sympathize with the Jews?

3. How did Leopold Socha show his respect not only for Jews as individuals but for the Jewish religion?

Working Together

Form a small group. Discuss the various reasons non-Jews gave for helping Jews escape the Nazis. Make a list of these reasons and share them with your class.

Active Learning

Writing a Script Imagine that you have been asked to write a script for a television series about non-Jews who helped Jews during the Holocaust. Work with three or four classmates. Together, choose one of the episodes from this case study for your script. First, outline the main events in the episode. Next, list and describe the characters you will include in your script. Then, choose one scene and write a first draft of a script. Remember, a script contains dialogue and descriptions of the scenes where the action takes place. Finally, revise your script and perform your scene for the class.

Lessons for Today

What responsibility do we have when it comes to helping someone in trouble? For example, what could we do when we see someone on the side of the road whose car has broken down? What should we do in a situation when helping someone else will put us at risk? What might happen to society if people stopped helping one another?

What Might You Have Done?

Imagine that you were a Dane during World War II, and the call went out to help the Jews escape to Sweden. Now imagine that you were a friend of Leopold Socha, and he asked you to help him feed the small group of Jews he was hiding. In which case do you think it would have been easier to help? Why?

CRITICAL THINKING
Refining Generalizations and Oversimplifications

Key Words

The following is a list of words that may signal a generalization or an oversimplification.

  all
  never
  always
  none
  no one
  everyone
  absolutely
  without a doubt

The following words can help refine or qualify a generalization or oversimplification.

  almost
  probably
  perhaps
  highly likely
  not very likely

You have probably heard statements such as these: "All politicians are corrupt." "No one understands." "They don't care." "None of them is any good." These statements are generalizations. A generalization is a broad statement that is meant to apply to many cases.

You have probably also heard statements such as these: "They should just close the street to traffic." "The two parties should just work together to solve the problem." These are examples of oversimplifications. An oversimplification is a statement that is only partly true. It does not give reasons or explore consequences.

As a critical thinker, you should avoid broad generalizations and oversimplifications in your thinking, reading, and writing. The following questions can help you refine or clarify your statements: What are the facts of the situation? How many specific cases have been examined to make this statement? Would this statement be true in every case? Are there any exceptions? What are they?

Copy the chart below into your notebook. Analyze the statements in the first column. Use Case Study 6 and your own reasoning ability to list the facts that would refine or clarify the statements. Finally, rewrite each statement to make it accurate.

Statement	What facts would refine or clarify this statement?
1. There was nobody in Poland who was willing to help the Jews	
2. All the people in France collaborated with the Nazis.	
3. None of the governments in the countries occupied by Germany was willing to take a stand against the Nazis to save the Jews living there.	

As news of the Nazi atrocities began to leak out of Germany, Jews around the world began to rise up in protest. At a New York protest in 1944, Rabbi Stephen S. Wise addressed a crowd of 100,000 people. The rabbi attacked the inaction of the U.S. government to Nazi brutalities.

WORLD REACTION TO THE HOLOCAUST

CRITICAL QUESTIONS

- Why do some people and nations "look the other way" when they see bad situations elsewhere in the world?
- What are the responsibilities of nations to the people of the world?

TERMS TO KNOW

- refugee
- quota
- Allied Powers
- War Refugee Board

ACTIVE LEARNING

After you have read this case study, you will be asked to write a newspaper editorial about how the United States and its allies reacted to the Holocaust. Pay careful attention to what the Allied Powers did and did not do to help the Jews. Look for Active Learning boxes to help you take notes as you read.

Zindel Grynszpan was born in a village in Poland in 1886. In 1911, he moved to Germany and settled in the city of Hanover. Zindel and his wife had three children and prospered in Germany.

On October 27, 1938, a German policeman came to the door. He ordered the family to come with him and take nothing but their passports. The Grynszpans were among the over 15,000 Polish-born Jews that the Nazis forced from their homes that day. They put the Jews in trucks and took them to the Polish border. As the truck left Hanover, the streets filled with people shouting that the Jews should get out of Germany.

When we reached the border, we were searched to see if anybody had any money, and anybody who had more than ten marks [4 dollars], the

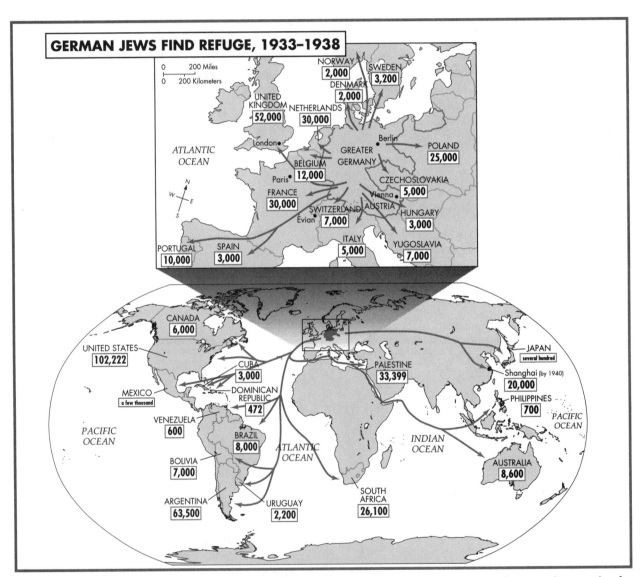

Of Europe's millions of Jews, only a fraction escaped the Holocaust. Between 1933 and 1938, thousands of German Jews found refuge in other countries. In which country in the Western Hemisphere did most German Jews find refuge? What do you suppose happened to the German Jews who escaped to countries such as Poland and Czechoslovakia?

balance was taken from him. . . . The Germans said, "You didn't bring any money into Germany and you can't take any more out."

The Grynszpans and other Jews then had to walk the last mile to the border.

The SS men were whipping us . . . and blood was flowing on the road. . . . They shouted at us: "Run, Run." I myself received a blow and I fell into a ditch. My son helped me and he said: "Run, run, dad—otherwise you'll die."

At first the Polish government refused to let the Jews into Poland. Like other countries in Europe and the Americas, Poland did not want to take in Jews. A major difference in this case, however, was that this group of Jews were Polish citizens. Poland had a legal duty to let them in.

Thousands of homeless people spent a bitterly cold night in no-man's-land between the two countries. Finally, the Polish government had to let them in. However, Nazi persecution continued to create more and more homeless Jews.

1 The Gates Slam Closed

After the Nazis came to power and began their campaign of persecution, Jews started to leave Germany. These Jews became **refugees.** A refugee is a person who has been forced to flee from his or her homeland for reasons of safety.

By 1938, over 150,000 Jewish refugees had fled Germany. In March 1938, Germany took over Austria. Suddenly more than 180,000 Austrian Jews found themselves under Nazi rule.

The German takeover of Austria meant that even more Jews had to find new homes. The question was where would these refugees go?

Limits on Immigration

During the 1930s, the United States had **quotas,** strict limits on immigration. Under those limits about 20,000 German Jews came to America between 1933 and 1937.

In 1938, President Franklin Roosevelt was under pressure at home in the United States to respond to the refugee problem. At the same time, the President knew there were strong anti-immigrant feelings in the United States. Public opinion polls also showed anti-Semitism was widespread. Because of these negative feelings, the President chose not to make major changes in U.S. immigration policy.

Great Britain admitted 60,000 Jews between 1933 and 1939. This was more than any other European country. Still, most Jews threatened by the Nazis could not find countries that would accept them.

The Evian Conference

Roosevelt arranged for a conference of 32 nations to discuss the problem of Jewish refugees. Countries from North America, South America, and Europe attended. Australia, New Zealand, and South Africa were also at the conference.

The conference met in July 1938, in the French resort town of Evian. With the exception of the Dominican Republic, no country stepped forward to help the Jewish refugees. Anti-immigrant feeling was strong in many countries. Economic times were bad, and jobs were scarce. There also was a great deal of anti-Semitism.

In the end, the United States told the Evian Conference that it would not increase its quota. Great Britain and France said they had no more room for immigrants. The Australian delegate said, "We don't have a racial problem and we don't want to import one." Canada said that when it came to accepting Jews, "none is too many."

One person who observed the conference was Golda Meir. Over 30 years later, she would become Prime Minister of Israel. In 1938, she represented the Jewish community in Palestine. "Palestine" was the name the Romans gave to ancient Judea when they drove most Jews from their homeland in the second century A.D. (See Case Study 1.) In 1938, Palestine was under

A Good Book to Read

In Kindling Flame: The Story of Hannah Senesh, 1921–1944, Linda Atkinson, New York: Shephard Books, 1985.

Hannah Senesh was born in Hungary in 1921. She immigrated to Palestine in 1939. In 1944, the Jewish community in Palestine sent 32 young people back to Europe to help rescue Jews. Hanna was one of two young women in the group. The Nazis captured Hannah and tortured her before executing her. This book tells her heroic story.

British control. Great Britain had restricted Jewish immigration to Palestine.

Golda Meir did what she could to change the minds of the delegates. She met with them in person. She spoke with them on the telephone. She spoke with newspaper reporters. But her efforts did not succeed. Golda Meir watched helplessly as the delegates explained how their countries had no room for the Jewish refugees.

The Evian Conference failed to change the policies of the countries that attended. As a result, over 100,000 Jewish refugees were left stranded.

The Gates Close Tighter

The Nazis paid close attention to the conference. When they saw that the world was unwilling to help the Jews, the Nazis increased the persecution. As you read earlier, in October 1938, the Nazis expelled over 15,000 Polish-born Jews from Germany. Then in November came Kristallnacht. (See Case Study 2.) Hundreds of thousands of German Jews began to leave Germany.

Most countries responded to the increased persecution by closing their doors completely. Others made it even harder for refugees to enter. One of the worst blows to Jewish refugees came from Great Britain. In May 1939, the British cut the number of Jews allowed into Palestine. Until 1939, most Jewish refugees from Europe went to Palestine. About 500,000 Jews were living there, rebuilding their national homeland.

However, the Arab population of the region opposed Jewish immigration. The British were concerned that the Arabs would side with the Germans if war came. To keep the Arabs on their side, the British set a quota. For many Jewish refugees, that strict quota became a death sentence.

Thinking It Over

1. What was the result of the Evian Conference?
2. Why did the British limit Jewish immigration to Palestine?

2 The Voyage of the *St. Louis*

European Jews tried desperately to escape from the Nazis. On May 13, 1939, the steamship *St. Louis* left Germany bound for Havana, Cuba. There were 936 hopeful passengers on board. All but six were Jewish refugees.

The passengers on the *St. Louis* came from all walks of life. Max Loewe was a successful lawyer traveling with his wife and two children. Gerda Weiss was a young dressmaker. Her boyfriend had told her that he would be waiting with a marriage license and a wedding ring.

Bruno Glade was a pianist. His wife and small children were waiting for him in Havana. The Guttmans were a newly married couple. Their trip on the *St. Louis* was a honeymoon as well as an escape from Nazi Germany. Mrs. Feilchenfeld was one of the busiest passengers. She was caring for her four little children while her husband waited for her in New York.

Bound for a New Life

All of the refugees had bought certificates from the Cuban government. The certificates would allow them to stay in Cuba. About 200 Jews expected to remain there. The rest had met the immigration requirements that permitted them to come to the United States.

However, the U.S.-bound refugees could not enter the United States right away. According to the quota system, they would have to wait between three months and three years for their turn. They expected to wait in Cuba, which is only 90 miles from the United States.

Captain Gustav Schroeder was in command of the *St. Louis*. He was a German. However, Captain Schroeder strongly opposed Nazi persecution of the Jews.

Entry Denied

The *St. Louis* arrived in Havana on May 27. A crowd of relatives and friends was on the dock waiting. Bruno Glade's family was there. So was Gerda Weiss's boyfriend.

However, only 22 passengers were allowed ashore. The Cuban government had canceled the landing certificates it had sold to the rest of the Jews. The Cuban president was demanding a huge bribe to let the Jews into Cuba.

Guards patrolled the dock to make sure no one either boarded or left the ship. At night, the Cubans used searchlights to make sure no one on the *St. Louis* swam ashore.

As quickly as possible, an American Jewish organization stepped in to negotiate with the Cubans. However, in the end it could not raise the money quickly enough to satisfy Cuba's corrupt president.

Newspapers in the United States ran front-page stories about what was happening in Cuba. However, the U.S. government refused to help.

On June 2, the Cubans forced the *St. Louis* to leave Cuba. Friends and relatives stood on the dock and watched helplessly as their loved ones sailed away.

Although the passengers were desperate, Captain Schroeder did not give up hope. He set a course that took the *St. Louis* close to the Florida coast. The ship was so close to land that the passengers could see the lights of the city of Miami.

"I'm Only A Very Little Jew."

Schroeder sailed slowly hoping a deal could be worked out. Perhaps a country in South America would take the refugees. Meanwhile, a U.S. Coast Guard ship followed the *St. Louis* to make sure no refugee jumped overboard and swam to shore.

Some Americans were angry that their government would not take in the refugees. Bishop James Cannon Jr., of Richmond, Virginia, wrote a letter to his local newspaper. He called what was happening "one of the most disgraceful things that has happened in American history." *The New York Times* wrote an editorial that said:

> *Helpless families . . . thrust over the Polish frontier . . . are hard for us to visualize. But these exiles floated by our own shores. . . . We can only hope that some hearts will soften and some refuge will be found. The cruise of the* St. Louis *cries to high heaven of man's inhumanity to man.*

Nothing helped. On June 6, Captain Schroeder set a course for Hamburg. The passengers set up a patrol on deck to prevent any suicides. The children on board invented a game in which Jews try to get past some guards at a barrier.

"Are you a Jew?" asked one of the guards.

"Yes," answered the child at the barrier.

"Jews not admitted," snapped the guard.

"Oh, please let me in. I'm only a very little Jew."

Active Learning: Take notes on what some Americans said about the U.S. government's refusal to admit the refugees on the *St. Louis*. If you agree with those Americans you might consider mentioning their arguments in your editorial.

As the *St. Louis* sailed for Germany, a Jewish organization in Europe finally worked out a deal. France, England, Holland, and Belgium agreed to divide up the refugees. In the end, only the 288 Jews allowed into England were safe. Most of the refugees sent to France, Belgium, and Holland later died in the Holocaust.

Thinking It Over

1. What was Captain Schroeder's attitude toward Nazi persecution of Jews?
2. What eventually happened to the Jews on the *St. Louis*?

3 Roosevelt, the Allies, and the Holocaust

The Evian Conference and the *St. Louis* episode occurred in 1938 before the United States entered World War II. The United States joined the **Allied Powers** in 1941. The Allied Powers, or Allies, were the nations that fought Germany and other countries during the war. The Allies included Britain, France, and Russia. Many Jews hoped that by entering the war, the United States would end the horrors of the Holocaust. But as one U.S. official noted, the actions taken were "late and little."

President Roosevelt Acts

In 1942, President Franklin Roosevelt received a letter from Rabbi Stephen S. Wise. Rabbi Wise was a leader of the Jewish community in the United States. He was also an old friend of the President.

Wise asked the President to meet with him and other Jewish leaders about what was happening in Europe to Jews. The meeting took place on December 8. It was the only time President Roosevelt met with Jewish leaders to discuss the Holocaust. Rabbi Wise told Roosevelt that "unless action is taken immediately, the Jews of . . . Europe are doomed."

The President was sympathetic. He said he was "very well acquainted with most of the facts you are now bringing to our attention." He also said that he had other proof of the horrors occurring in Europe.

On December 17, Roosevelt had the U.S. government make a public statement about Germany's campaign to exterminate the Jews. Along with Great Britain and the Soviet Union, the United States issued a "declaration of solemn protest." This declaration by the Allies informed the world of what the Nazis were doing to the Jews, but it did nothing to stop the Nazis.

War Refugee Board

Not until early 1944 did the President take any serious action to help the Jews of Europe. It came after a meeting on January 16 with Henry Morgenthau, a member of his cabinet. Morgenthau, who was Jewish, told the President that the United States had done nothing to help the Jews of Europe. Worse than that, certain branches of the government actually had hidden information about the situation.

Roosevelt realized that a scandal would erupt if word got out to the public. Several days after the meeting with Morgenthau, the President set up the **War Refugee Board** (WRB). The board worked to help Jewish refugees and to protect Jews in countries allied with Germany. However, by the time U.S. support for the Jews of Europe came, most of the damage had already been done.

Auschwitz and the Allies

After President Roosevelt set up the WRB, he faced the question of whether or not to bomb Auschwitz. During the spring and summer of 1944, Jewish groups in the United States repeatedly asked that Auschwitz be bombed. Each day up to 10,000 people were being murdered in its gas chambers.

After May 1944, the United States had opportunities to bomb Auschwitz. U.S. warplanes had driven the Germans from the sky. In June and July, U.S. bombers flew over the railroad lines leading to Auschwitz.

Bombing the railroad lines would have slowed the deportation of Jews to the death camp. However, the bombers' orders were to hit German oil refining factories less than 50 miles from Auschwitz.

On August 20 and September 13, American bombers attacked German factories *inside* Auschwitz. (See Going to the Source, p. 97) These raids hit targets less than five miles

The steamship St. Louis waited off the Florida coast with 936 Jewish refugees from Germany. The passengers were desperate for permission to enter the United States. That permission did not come. In June 1938, the ship returned to Europe. Most of its passengers later died in the Holocaust. The Roman Catholic bishop of Richmond called the episode "one of the most disgraceful things that has happened in American history."

from the Auschwitz gas chambers and crematoria. These were only a few of the many U.S. bombing attacks on targets near the Auschwitz death camp. The U.S. government knew the role Auschwitz played in the Final Solution. Yet neither the gas chambers nor the crematoria were ever bombed.

Why didn't the United States bomb the death camps? One reason was that U.S. military planners decided that civilian matters would not interfere with strictly military goals. One of them said, "We are over there to win the war and not to take care of refugees." However, Allied military did help civilians involving Greeks, Poles, and Yugoslavs.

Although President Roosevelt was concerned about the Jews of Europe, he believed that the best way to save the Jews was to defeat Germany and end the war.

Neither the United States nor its allies did very much to save the Jews from the Holocaust. It was a moral challenge that they failed to meet.

In the end, one of the four crematoria at Auschwitz was blown up. The job was done by

Active Learning: Take notes on the U.S. response to the Holocaust. What did the U.S. government do to help the Jews of Europe? In your editorial, give your opinion of each action.

a group of Jewish inmates at the camp. They gathered dynamite and weapons and blew up the crematorium on October 7, 1944. In an hour-long battle that followed, the group also killed three German soldiers and wounded about a dozen more before being wiped out.

Liberating the Death Camps

The liberation of the death camps and concentration camps began in July 1944, when the Soviet army entered the Maidanek death camp. The Soviets liberated Auschwitz in January

Only a few Germans were held accountable for the horrors of the Holocaust. Here, a Russian Jew who had been a slave laborer points out a German guard who had brutally beat prisoners. The camp had been liberated by the U.S. Third Armored Division.

GOING TO THE SOURCE

Bombing Auschwitz

On September 13, 1944, the U.S. Air Force bombed the Buna factory, a rubber factory located in Auschwitz III. Although the gas chambers and transport lines were within striking range, the U.S. military refused to destroy them. Below is a military photo showing the bombs dropping on Buna. The quote below the photo was made by author Elie Wiesel, a teenager at Auschwitz at the time.

Source: Dino Brugioni/National Archives, Washington, D.C.

Elie Wiesel and other inmates of Auschwitz heard the Allied bombs dropping around them that day. Wiesel recalled:

We began to hear the airplanes. Almost at once the barracks began to shake. "They're bombing Buna," someone shouted. I thought of my father [who worked as a slave laborer at the factory]. But I was glad all the same. To see the whole works go up in fire—what revenge! . . . We were not afraid. And yet, if a bomb had fallen on the blocks [where the prisoners lived], it alone would have claimed hundreds of victims on the spot. But we no longer were afraid of death; at any rate not of that death. Every bomb that exploded filled us with joy and gave us new confidence in life.

From Elie Wiesel as quoted in Michael Berenbaum, *The World Must Know.* Boston: Little Brown, 1993, p. 145.

1. Although there was a chance that Wiesel's father was working at the Buna factory, Wiesel was still glad that the factory was being destroyed. Why do you think he felt that way?

2. Why weren't Wiesel and other inmates afraid of being killed by one of the bombs?

Liberated prisoners at the Mauthausen slave labor camp near Linz, Austria, give a rousing welcome to the soldiers of the U.S. 11th Armored Division on May 6, 1945. The sign at top, which "salutes the anti-fascist forces" was created by Spanish prisoners at the camp.

1945. American and British forces first reached concentration camps in April of that year.

Despite what people had heard or read, the Allied soldiers could not believe the horrors they saw. One U.S. soldier described how his division reacted when they saw the condition of the people in the Nordhausen camp.

> *Oh the odors, well there is no way to describe the odors.... Many of the boys I am talking about now—these were tough soldiers, there were combat men who had been all the way through on the invasion—were ill and vomiting, throwing up, just at the sight of this.*

One journalist wrote, "You can't understand it, even when you've seen it." A British officer told the Nazi commander of the Bergen-Belsen concentration camp, "You've made a fine hell here."

Most of the survivors that the soldiers found were little more than skeletons. Thousands died despite the soldiers' efforts to save them. At Bergen-Belsen, the death rate of Jews *after* liberation was 300 per day.

The Nuremberg Trials

Back in the winter of 1943, the Allied Powers decided that when the war ended they would put German leaders on trial for their crimes. Within two weeks of Germany's surrender in 1945, the Allies agreed to hold the trials in the German city of Nuremberg. Finally, Nazi Germany would have to answer for what it had done. For the victims of the Holocaust, however, these trials would serve as small compensation for the horrors and losses they had endured.

Thinking It Over

1. What did President Roosevelt do in response to his meeting with Henry Morgenthau?
2. What was the U.S. military's position on bombing Auschwitz?

Case Study Review

Identifying Main Ideas

1. Why didn't Captain Schroeder immediately head back to Europe after Cuba refused to allow the *St. Louis* to dock?

2. What was the result of the Evian Conference?

3. What was President Roosevelt's attitude toward bombing Auschwitz? Do you agree or disagree with him? Explain your opinion.

Working Together

Form a small group with three classmates. Write several newspaper headlines about the Evian Conference and the voyage of the *St. Louis*. Make a bulletin board display of your headlines. You may wish to illustrate your headlines or write articles to accompany them.

Active Learning

Writing an Editorial An editorial is used to express a writer's opinion. However, that opinion must be based on facts and evidence. Write an editorial expressing your opinion about the U.S. response to the Holocaust.

Lessons for Today

There are conflicts within and between countries around the globe. These conflicts threaten the lives of many people. What obligation do you think the United States has today to help other nations and people around the world? Keep in mind that in many cases, helping to solve problems could be very expensive or put American lives in danger.

What Might You Have Done?

Imagine that you are at the Evian Conference. After listening to the delegates tell you that their countries have no room for Jewish refugees, you are given the opportunity to make a short speech. What would you say to the representatives at the conference to convince them to open their doors? What would you say to convince your own country to open its doors?

CRITICAL THINKING

Analyzing the Allies' Actions During the Holocaust

The Language of Thinking

Analyzing is part of the learning process. When you analyze something, you break it into its parts in order to examine it more closely. Analyzing information allows you to understand situations or issues better.

Actions are things that people do. Policies are plans, rules, or beliefs that guide people's actions. Before a group takes action, it must decide what actions are possible. It must consider the reasons for those actions. It also must consider the consequences of those actions. Finally, it must consider the value or importance of those actions.

Read the paragraphs below and answer the questions that follow.

Between 1933 and 1939, the Germans did not hide the fact that they were removing Jews from Germany. Newspapers in Allied countries reported the deportations and other unfair acts against the Jews. However, these stories did not appear often. Some Allied reporters in Germany were afraid to report what they saw and heard. Some U.S. publishers did not believe the stories were true. They did not allow the stories to be printed.

The Allies did not take steps to stop Germany's actions. Many Jews tried to leave German-occupied countries to go to Great Britain and to the United States. However, both countries had quotas that limited the number of Jews they would accept.

In January 1942, the Nazis developed a plan they called the Final Solution. They would kill *all* the Jews. Germany tried to keep the killings a secret. However, news of the Final Solution leaked to Great Britain in the spring of 1942. Later that year, the United States confirmed that the reports were true. Still, for two more years, the Allies took almost no action. They warned the Germans that their crimes would be punished. However, the Allies did not allow more refugees to enter their countries. Nor did they bomb the death camps in Poland.

After the Allies defeated Germany in 1945, they realized they had waited too long. Six million Jews were dead.

1. What are some actions that the Allies might have taken to help the Jews?

2. What would be the reason for each action?

3. What might have been the consequences of each action?

4. Why would each action have been important?

Finally brought to justice for her crimes, Dr. Herta Oberhauser, a Nazi doctor hears her sentence of 20 years in prison. She was found guilty of brutal experiments on death camp prisoners.

ADOLF EICHMANN ON TRIAL

CRITICAL QUESTIONS

- How did the world attempt to punish those responsible for the Holocaust?
- How did Nazis try to justify their crimes?

TERMS TO KNOW

- tribunal
- aggression
- prosecute
- defendant
- acquit

ACTIVE LEARNING

As you read this case study, note how Nazis such as Adolf Eichmann justified their actions. Also pay attention to how the Allies and the Israelis rejected the Nazis' excuses for their crimes. After you read this case study, you will be asked to write a scene for a play about a trial of a Nazi. Look for Active Learning boxes to help you take notes for your scene.

May 11, 1960, was a cold winter night in Argentina. It was about 7:30 in the evening in Buenos Aires, the country's capital.

A car with its hood open was parked near the corner of Garibaldi Street. A small house stood a few feet from the car.

One man was tinkering with the car's engine. A second man seemed to be helping him. Two other men waited inside the car.

There was nothing wrong with the car. Nor was anything wrong with a second car parked with its hood raised around the corner. The men with the two cars were secret agents of the State of Israel. They were waiting for a man who called himself Ricardo Klement to return to his home on Garibaldi Street.

Finally, at 8:05 a bus stopped and a thin, balding, middle-aged man got off. It was hard to see him clearly in the dark.

As the man approached the corner of Garibaldi Street, an Israeli in the second car whispered, "Someone's coming, but I can't see who it is." Then came a second excited whisper, "It's him!"

The driver immediately switched on his headlights. This was to blind Klement so that he would not see the second car. The men feared Klement was carrying a gun.

As Klement reached the car, one of the agents sprang at him. The two men fell to the ground. Klement screamed. One agent grabbed Klement's legs while the other grabbed his hands. Within seconds Klement and the Israelis were in the back seat of the car.

Less than an hour later the car arrived at a specially prepared hideout. The agents searched their prisoner carefully and then began questioning him. "What is your name?"

"Ricardo Klement," came the answer.

"What is your real name?" the agent asked.

"Otto Heninger," the man finally answered.

"Were your SS numbers 45326 and 63752?"

"Yes."

"Then tell me your real name!"

"My name is Adolf Eichmann."

The four Israelis did not say a word. They finally had captured the man who organized the deportment of millions of Jews to the Nazi death camps. They stared at him with horror and hatred. But they did not hurt him. Their job now was to keep him alive and smuggle him from Argentina to Israel. There, Eichmann would stand trial for his crimes against the Jewish people.

1 The Nuremberg Trials

In the last days of the war, leaders of the Nazi government attempted to avoid being captured and tried for their crimes. Some of them followed Hitler's example and committed suicide. Joseph Goebbels, chief of propaganda, committed suicide with his family. Heinrich Himmler, head of the SS, committed suicide when British soldiers captured him.

In August 1945, the Allies formed the International Military Tribunal (IMT) to bring the Nazi leaders to trial. A **tribunal** is a court of justice. Twenty-two Nazi leaders went on trial before the IMT.

The highest-ranking Nazi official at the trial was Hermann Goering. He had been one of Hitler's closest associates. In July 1941, Goering had ordered Reinhard Heydrich to organize the Final Solution. The men on trial were among the most important Nazi officials and military leaders.

One Nazi official who was not at Nuremberg was Adolf Eichmann. He slipped through Allied hands and disappeared.

The German leaders were tried for three categories of crimes. The first was "crimes against peace." This meant planning and carrying out a war of **aggression.** Aggression is an attack on somebody.

The second category was "war crimes." This meant breaking the rules of war. It included killing prisoners of war and destroying homes and property.

The third category of crimes was called "crimes against humanity." These crimes included the mass murder of civilian populations. The Nazi campaign to exterminate the Jewish people was covered under this category.

Symbols of Racial Hatred

Justice Reinhard Jackson headed the American team **prosecuting** the Nazi leaders. To prosecute is to take legal steps against someone. Justice Jackson was a member of the U.S. Supreme Court. In his opening statement, Justice Jackson called the Nazi leaders "the living symbols of racial hatred, of terrorism and violence, and of the arrogance and cruelty of power."

The trial lasted from November 1945 until October 1946. Twelve **defendants** were sentenced to death. A defendant is a person who is on trial for a crime. One of them, Hermann Goering, committed suicide before he could be executed. Seven others received life imprisonment or long prison sentences. Three men were **acquitted,** or cleared of the charges against them.

Later Trials

The first Nuremberg trial was followed by a dozen others. In those trials between 1946 and 1949, 177 defendants were accused of various crimes. The defendants included doctors who did the selections at the death camps or performed horrible medical experiments. The Allies also tried officers of the Einsatzgruppen. Businessmen who used slave laborers, officials who ran concentration camps, and others who helped carry out the Final Solution also went on trial.

This photograph shows some of the 22 Nazi leaders who were brought to trial for war crimes and crimes against humanity at Nuremberg. Seated in the front row at left is Hermann Goering, one of Hitler's closest associates. Goering and 11 other Nazis were sentenced to death.

Many of the defendants in the Nuremberg trials said they were innocent because they were only following orders. The judges strongly rejected this excuse. They insisted that all individuals are responsible for what they do. Orders that break basic moral codes should not be followed, even if they come from a government. This idea was one of the most important principles to come out of the Nuremberg war crimes trials.

Active Learning: Take notes on how the Nazis defended themselves and why their defense was not accepted. You will see a similar defense when you read about the Eichmann trial.

Most of the defendants in the second round of trials were convicted. Some were sentenced to death. However, in 1948, many of the death sentences were reduced to prison sentences. In 1951, the sentences were reduced again. Many of the convicted war criminals were freed after only a few years in prison.

Why was this done? The main reason was because by the late 1940s there was great tension between the United States and the Soviet Union. With the Soviet Union as an enemy, the United States thought it needed the support of the German people. The United States believed that shortening the sentences of former Nazi leaders might help win that support. The decision was a great disappointment to the survivors of the Holocaust.

DeNazification

In 1945, the Allies had planned to "deNazify" Germany. To do so they planned to find more than 100,000 people guilty of Holocaust crimes and put them on trial. However, "deNazification" slowed to a halt because of tension between Communist Soviet Union and the Western democracies of the United States, Britain, and France.

The four former allies had divided Germany into four portions after the war. In 1949, the United States, Britain, and France united their portions and set up a new German state called West Germany. The new state was a democracy. Yet, it did little to bring former Nazi officials to justice.

Results of Nuremberg

The Nuremberg trials were extremely important because they told the world in great detail about the Holocaust. The trials also established the principle that individuals cannot avoid responsibility for their actions by saying they had to follow orders. At Nuremberg, leaders of a government were held responsible for what they did while in power. The judgments at Nuremberg also set standards for judging the actions of nations in the future.

However, it is also true that most of the Nazi war criminals escaped justice. They went back to their old lives in Germany or fled to other countries. Many became successful and held prominent positions after the war. Some took on new identities. Others kept their real names.

Thinking It Over

1. What were "crimes against humanity?"
2. Why were many of the sentences given to Nazi war criminals reduced?

2 Bringing Adolf Eichmann to Justice

When World War II ended, David Ben-Gurion was the leader of the Jewish community in Palestine. One day in 1945, he spoke to a small group of his closest advisers. He pounded his fist on a table. "Adolf Eichmann," he said. "That's the man who *must* be brought to justice if he is still alive."

Adolf Eichmann was not one of the leaders of the Nazi party. However, once Hitler decided to exterminate the Jews, no Nazi official did more to carry out that policy than Adolf Eichmann.

Eichmann rose through the ranks of the SS because he worked hard and with great enthusiasm. He made his first mark as an excellent organizer in persecuting Jews after

Adolf Eichmann did more to carry out Hitler's extermination policy than perhaps any other Nazi official. Here, he is shown as a young Nazi officer.

Germany took over Austria in 1938. During 1938 and 1939, Eichmann was in charge of forcing Jews out of Austria.

He headed the effort that drove over 100,000 Jews out of Austria in less than two years. Eichmann made sure that his men seized all the property of the Jews before they left. "It all went like an assembly line," he often boasted. A Jewish leader who dealt with Eichmann described how Eichmann's system worked.

> *You put in a Jew at one end, with property, a shop, a bank account, and legal rights. He . . . came out the other end without property, without . . . rights, with nothing except a passport and orders to leave the country within a fortnight; otherwise he would find himself inside a concentration camp.*

Eichmann enjoyed his work. He added his own personal cruelty to his victims' suffering whenever he could. He regularly lied to leaders of the Jewish community. He used nasty and vulgar insults when talking to them. Eichmann liked showing Jews the power he had over their lives.

Eichmann's work won him promotions every year after 1937. In 1941, he became an SS lieutenant colonel. He held that rank until the end of the war.

Eichmann was the official who organized the Wannsee Conference for his boss Reinhard Heydrich. (See Case Study 4.) He also prepared a record of the conference. After World War II, that record played an important role in the trials of Nazi war criminals.

Organizing Mass Murder

Between 1942 and 1945, Eichmann was in charge of deporting Jews from all over Europe to the death camps. He determined the timing and pace of the deportations. His job also included seizing Jewish property and hiding the real purpose of the deportations from the outside world.

Eichmann did his murderous job with the same skill and enthusiasm he showed before the war. Heinrich Himmler, the head of the SS, called Eichmann "the master" when it came to deporting Jews.

"The master" was completely dedicated to his work. He often visited concentration camps and death camps. Eichmann visited the Chelmno death camp to check the new system of execution by gassing. He also visited the Treblinka death camp.

In 1944, Eichmann went to Auschwitz. He made suggestions to speed up the process of murder. Eichmann wanted to increase the murder rate from 10,000 to 12,000 per day. Eichmann also went to Hungary in 1944 to oversee the deportation of Jews to Auschwitz. He stopped at nothing to secure every available train. He did not care that the German army needed trains to get soldiers and weapons to the front lines. Like Hitler, Eichmann considered killing Jews to be more important than the needs of the German army.

Despite all efforts, Eichmann still could not get enough trains to deport all the Hungarian Jews. He therefore organized death marches out of Hungary. The marches resulted in the deaths of thousands of people.

Escaping Justice

After the war, many Nazi leaders escaped justice by fleeing Germany. Some went to Arab countries in the Middle East that were enemies of the State of Israel. Another escape route was called the "Rat Line." It led from Germany to Italy and from there to South America. Whether they used the "Rat Line" or other routes, most Nazis who fled Germany ended up in South America.

The fleeing Nazis got help from an organization of former SS members called ODESSA. They also received help from pro-Nazi Roman Catholic priests in several cities in Italy. Rome became the most important hideout for escaping Nazis.

Adolf Eichmann was one of the many Nazi war criminals who escaped to South America. He hid in Germany until 1950. That year, Eichmann made it to Argentina.

Tracking Down Eichmann

Eichmann had covered his tracks very effectively. For a while, not even his wife and children knew he was alive. Eventually, he was able to contact his wife and bring his family to Argentina.

The hunt for Eichmann began in 1945. The people who hunted Eichmann included members of the Jewish community in Palestine and Jews in Europe working with Simon Wiesenthal. Wiesenthal is a Holocaust survivor. After the war, he devoted his life to finding Nazis and bringing them to justice.

In 1948, the Jewish community in Palestine declared itself the State of Israel. Immediately, it was attacked by six Arab countries. Israel struggled to survive and build a new society. Although it put its plans to find Eichmann on hold, the Israeli government never gave up the idea of finding Nazi criminals who had escaped justice.

Meanwhile, Simon Wiesenthal was busy trailing Eichmann. During the 1950s, he found out that Eichmann was living in Argentina. He shared the information he collected with Israeli officials.

By 1959, the Israelis learned that Eichmann was using the name Ricardo Klement. They also had an address in Buenos Aires. But they had to be positive that Ricardo Klement was their man.

A Good Book To Read

The House on Garibaldi Street, by Isser Harel, Bantam Books, New York, 1975.

The hunt for Adolf Eichmann lasted from 1945 to 1960. Head of the Israeli Secret Services Isser Harel tells about the last successful stage of that hunt. *The House on Garibaldi Street* is a gripping eye-witness account of the capture of Adolf Eichmann.

In 1960, the Israelis sent an agent to Argentina to get a photograph of Klement. By then the Klement family lived on Garibaldi Street. The Israeli agent soon identified "Mrs. Klement" as Mrs. Eichmann. Identifying Ricardo Klement as Adolf Eichmann was more difficult. Finally, on a Sunday morning the agent was able to take a picture of Klement as he was gardening.

Back in Israel, the photograph was shown to people who had met Eichmann before 1945. A police expert then compared the photo with an old photo of Eichmann. The conclusion was that Ricardo Klement was almost definitely Adolf Eichmann.

In April 1960, the Israeli agents arrived in Argentina. They spent weeks learning Eichmann's daily routine. The Israelis decided that their best chance was to grab Eichmann when he came home from work.

As you have read, Eichmann was captured and taken to an Israeli hideout for ten days. He was then secretly put on a plane. The plane took off five minutes after midnight on May 21. It delivered Eichmann to Israel on May 22, 1960.

Thinking It Over

1. What was Eichmann's role in the Holocaust?
2. How did the Israeli agents capture Eichmann?

3 The Trial of Adolf Eichmann

On April 11, 1961, at 9:00 A.M. Adolf Eichmann walked into a courtroom in Jerusalem, Israel. For his own protection he sat in a bulletproof glass booth.

Eichmann's trial was different from the Nuremberg trials in one important way. At Nuremberg, the Nazi crimes against the Jews were part of the Nazi "crimes against humanity" and "war crimes."

However, the main focus of the Eichmann trial was "crimes against the Jewish people." The man on trial in Jerusalem had been concerned with only *one* goal during the war. That goal had been the extermination of the Jewish people.

Eichmann's lawyer argued that the State of Israel had no right to try Eichmann. He said Eichmann could not get a fair trial in Israel from its Jewish judges.

The Israeli judges explained that when a judge sits in a courtroom, he or she still had human feelings. However, a judge's job is to control those feelings. Otherwise, "no judge would ever be qualified to sit in judgment" in cases involving murder or other terrible crimes.

The judges agreed that the Holocaust "shocks every Jew to the core." But it was their

Adolf Eichmann conducted his defense from behind a bullet proof glass booth. His main defense was that he was following orders.

GOING TO THE SOURCE

Gideon Hausner's Summation at the Trial of Adolf Eichmann

Gideon Hausner was the chief prosecutor at the trial of Adolf Eichmann in 1961. Below is part of what he said at the conclusion of the trial in his summation speech to the judges.

For two months the survivors of this terrible Holocaust have taken their places on the witness stand and given their testimony. . . . We were shocked to hear of murder, brutality, tortures and atrocities [cruelties] which, had they not been described by living men and women, it would have been impossible to believe they were perpetrated [committed] by human beings.

All these things have been heard by the man in the glass dock. It might have been expected that today at least . . . he would utter one word of regret. . . . Instead, he has declared that he does not believe in regret.

We saw him . . . denying facts that cry out from every piece of evidence, searching for excuses . . . every one of which was designed to cover up his own liability [responsibility] for the ocean of blood that has been spilled. To achieve this, he has been ready to deny his own statements, to recant [take back] his own confessions, to claim that documents have been forged, that witnesses—even his own testimony—are mistaken, that reports are false.

Truth and falsehood no longer have any normal meaning for such men. Truth is whatever serves their purpose. Falsehood is whatever hinders [blocks] them. If there is regret in their hearts, it is because their loathsome [horrible] work was not completed.

[Carrying out the Holocaust] was . . . an act of will, deliberate and conscious. On the part of the gang of criminals who came to power it was also a matter of . . . careful calculation.

From Gideon Hausner, *Justice in Jerusalem*, New York: Harper and Row, 1966, pp. 388–90.

1. According to Hausner, how did Eichmann react to the charges against him?
2. What did Hausner say about the meaning of truth and falsehood for people like Eichmann?

duty to judge Eichmann fairly. "This duty we shall discharge," they said firmly.

"I Do Not Stand Alone."

The prosecutor for the State of Israel was Gideon Hausner. His opening statement began:

> As I stand before you, Judges of Israel . . . I do not stand alone. With me . . . stand six million accusers. But they cannot rise to their feet and point an accusing finger toward the man who sits in the glass dock and cry: "I accuse." For their ashes were piled up in the hills of Auschwitz and in the fields of Treblinka, or washed away by the rivers of Poland; their graves are scattered over the length and breadth of Europe.

Hausner added, "It falls to me to be their spokesman."

Hausner also said that Eichmann would be given the right that he had denied every "single one of his victims." That right was to defend himself in court.

He ended his opening statement with the last verse of a lullaby composed in the Vilna ghetto.

> For the ocean has its limits,
> Prisons have their walls around,
> But our suffering and torment
> Have no limit and no bound.

Hausner called 112 witnesses to document the Holocaust and Eichmann's role in it. Often what they described was too much for people to bear. Survivors sitting in the audience sobbed and fainted. Reporters walked out of the courtroom when they could stand no more.

Yehiel Dinur, a well-known writer, had survived and written about Auschwitz. He described a place so different from the normal world that he called it "planet Auschwitz" and the "ashen planet." Dinur spoke of his writing and the "vow I swore" to Auschwitz victims to tell the world what happened there. Suddenly, Dinur could not go on. His entire body trembled. Suddenly he collapsed. It took him two weeks to recover.

Eichmann's Defense

Eichmann's main defense was that he was following orders. He said he had no power of his own. "I never took decisions by myself," he testified. "I never did anything, great or small, without obtaining in advance . . . instructions from my superiors." Many of his answers were, "It was so ordered."

Eichmann's other line of defense was to lie. He lied about how much authority he had, about what he knew, and about what he did. He even denied he was an anti-Semite.

Active Learning: Take notes on the accusations against Eichmann and how he defended himself. Later you might include some of this material in your scene.

Eichmann's Sentence

On December 11, 1961, the Israeli court found Adolf Eichmann guilty of "crimes against the Jewish people, crimes against humanity, war crimes, and membership in criminal organizations." Four days later it sentenced him to death. Eichmann appealed the court's decision, but the court of appeals upheld the guilty verdict. In May 1962, Eichmann was hanged and his body cremated. His ashes were scattered at sea. He is the only person ever executed by the State of Israel.

Thinking It Over

1. In accusing Eichmann, what did Gideon Hausner mean when he said, "I do not stand alone"?
2. How did Eichmann defend his actions?

Case Study Review

Identifying Main Ideas

1. (a) What were the Nuremberg trials? (b) For what three categories of crimes were Nazi leaders tried?
2. Why did David Ben-Gurion want to capture Adolf Eichmann?
3. In what way was the focus of the Eichmann trial different from the focus of the Nuremberg trials?

Working Together

Form a small group. Make a list that summarizes the crimes that Adolf Eichmann committed between 1938 and 1945. Then make a time line that shows Eichmann's crimes, his departure to Argentina, and his capture and trial.

 ### Active Learning

Writing a Scene Review the notes you took as you read this case study. Identify the material that a prosecutor could use in a trial for crimes that the Nazis committed during the Holocaust. Also, locate material about how the Nazis on trial attempted to defend themselves. Use that material to write a short scene for a movie. You may want to include a judge in your scene as well as a prosecutor, a defendant, and witnesses.

Lessons for Today

An important principle that emerged from both the Nuremberg and Eichmann trials is that individuals are responsible for their actions. Individuals cannot hide behind the defense that they were ordered to do something, even if that order came from a government.

Think of actions taken by governments in the world today. Are there any actions that you think people should refuse to carry out? What risks are involved when people refuse to carry out orders? Do you think that most people are prepared to say no to orders that they believe are morally wrong?

What Might You Have Done?

Imagine that you were one of the men who captured Adolf Eichmann. How do you think you might have felt? What questions would you have asked him?

CRITICAL THINKING

Examining Responsibility for the Holocaust

Throughout our lives, we evaluate behavior. We decide whether a certain action is good or bad, right or wrong. An action that we decide is good or right is a moral action. In judging whether an action is moral, we consider factors such as the following:

- What are the circumstances?
- What are the rules or laws, if any?
- What is the right thing to do?
- What is the wrong thing to do?

Opinions may differ about a certain behavior. Some people may think a certain behavior is moral. Some may think it is immoral, or not moral. Some may think it is neither moral nor immoral.

In your notebook, list some of the different kinds of behavior, such as giving spare change or food to a homeless person or avoiding or disliking someone who looks different from you. You can list actions you have seen others do, as well as actions you have done yourself.

When you have completed your list, copy the graphic organizer below into your notebook. Use the organizer to describe

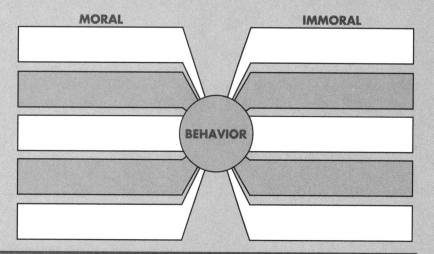

you think are immoral. Compare your completed organizer with someone else's. How are they alike? How are they different?

DISCUSSION

Use your own ideas and what you have learned about the Holocaust to have a class discussion about the questions below. Remember the rules of debate. Allow each person a turn. Listen carefully. You may want to take notes during the discussion.

1. What kind of behavior should be allowed in war? Explain your answer.

2. How should a government treat its citizens? Should it protect all citizens or just some? Explain your answer.

3. Should SS officials who said that they followed Hitler's orders be held responsible for the murder of the Jews? Give your reasons.

4. Should people who did nothing to help the Jews be held morally responsible for murder? Give your reasons.

5. What would you do in a situation in which you knew something was wrong?

Weary from their long voyage on the crowded S.S. Exodus and concerned by Britain's refusal to let them remain in Palestine, Jewish mothers wait on the docks in the city of Haifa in 1947.

REMEMBERING THE HOLOCAUST

CRITICAL QUESTIONS

■ Why is it important to remember the Holocaust?

■ How can the memory of the Holocaust best be preserved?

TERMS TO KNOW

■ exodus

■ displaced person

■ Aliya Bet

■ Zionism

ACTIVE LEARNING

In this follow-up chapter, you will read about the survivors of the Holocaust. You will find out where they went, what they did, and how they coped with their past. After you are finished, you will be asked to write a newspaper article about people who survived the Holocaust. As you read, note the problems that survivors faced after being liberated from the Nazi death camps and concentration camps.

In July 1947, an old four-deck steamship left France. Its destination was the city of Haifa in Palestine. Squeezed on board were 4,500 passengers. They did not mind the crowded conditions on the ship. They were used to much worse. These passengers were Holocaust survivors. They were sailing to join the growing Jewish community in Palestine. There they hoped to rebuild their shattered lives.

Their ship's name was *Exodus*. The ship was named after the book of the Bible that tells how the ancient Israelites escaped from slavery in Egypt and went to the land of Israel. An **exodus** also means "the departure of a large number of people."

The Jews on board the *Exodus* were sailing to the very same land where their ancestors had lived over 3,000 years earlier. However, in 1947 that land was called Palestine and was under British control.

The British had strict limits on the number of Jews allowed to immigrate to Palestine. Yet there were several hundred thousand Jewish refugees in Europe with no place to go.

Most of the refugees wanted to go to Palestine. They were prepared to sneak into Palestine illegally if necessary.

Between 1945 and 1947, over 85 ships sailed for Palestine. The British navy stopped most of them. The British put the Jews in camps on the island of Cyprus. These camps were enclosed by barbed wire and had armed guards. They reminded the survivors of the concentration camps.

Four British warships trailed the *Exodus* from the start of its journey. When the *Exodus* got close to Haifa, British sailors boarded it.

The Jews fought back. The British used machine guns, killing three Jews and wounding over 100. The ship itself was damaged in the fight.

The Exodus is shown in Haifa harbor during a 1942 trip to Palestine. The sign refers to a militant group, the Haganah, which sponsored bringing Jewish refugees to Palestine as well as taking military action against the British.

Jews Murdered in European Countries During the Holocaust

Country	Number of Jews Murdered	Percentage of the Jewish Population They Made Up
Austria	40,000	20%
Belgium	40,000	67%
Czechoslovakia	315,000	88%
Denmark	130	2%
Estonia	1,500	33%
France	90,000	30%
Germany	170,000	32%
Greece	60,000	80%
Hungary	200,000	50%
Italy	8,000	16%
Latvia	80,000	84%
Lithuania	217,000	97%
Luxembourg	700	23%
Netherlands	105,000	75%
Poland	2,850,000	88%
Romania	425,000	50%
Soviet Union	1,252,000	44%
Yugoslavia	60,000	80%

Source: Simon Wiesenthal Center, "36 Questions Often Asked About the Holocaust," Revised Edition, 1989.

Never before the Holocaust had such a slaughter been carried out against a people. In some countries, almost the entire Jewish population was wiped out. In which countries were two thirds or more of the Jews murdered? Other countries were affected less. Why do you think the toll in Denmark somewhat low?

Railings were ripped off and oil stained the decks. There were gashes on both sides of the boat.

The British had decided to take a hard line with illegal Jewish immigrants. Instead of taking the Jews to Cyprus, they put the Jews on prison boats and sent them back to France.

But the Jews refused to get off the boats in France. They went on a hunger strike. The British then sailed their prison boats to the German port of Hamburg. Once again the Jews refused to leave the boats. The British used tear gas, hoses, and clubs to drive the Holocaust survivors off the boats. They then imprisoned the Jews in a **displaced persons** (DP) camp in Germany. A displaced person is a refugee with no home to which to return.

The *Exodus* incident won worldwide sympathy for the Jewish refugees. Equally important, the *Exodus* itself became a symbol of the determination of Holocaust survivors to rebuild their lives.

1 The Extent of the Holocaust

There is no way to know exactly how many Jews died during the Holocaust. The best estimate is 6 million people.

However, the real number may be higher. In 1941, the Einsatzgruppen killed thousands of infants and babies before their births were recorded. Thousands more people in isolated villages were deported from their homes without being counted.

Overall the Nazis killed nearly two-thirds of the Jews in Europe and one-third of all the Jews in the world. Over 4,500 Jewish communities in Europe were wiped out. Hundreds of smaller communities disappeared without anyone recording exactly how or when they were destroyed.

The Holocaust also wiped out the Jewish culture of Eastern Europe. For centuries, Eastern Europe had been the cultural and spiritual center of world Jewry. Before the Holocaust, Eastern Europe had the largest Jewish population in the world. By 1945, that world was gone. Only the ashes of the dead and the memories of the survivors remained.

Displaced Persons

The end of World War II ended the Nazi execution of Jews. But it did not provide a new start for tens of thousands of Holocaust survivors. These survivors became displaced persons.

Most of the Jewish displaced persons came from Poland. In 1945, there were about 65,000 of them in Germany. The Allies placed them in overcrowded camps. While no one starved, conditions in the camps were very poor.

Yet these Jews did not want to go back to Poland, which had become a huge graveyard for their people. Ninety percent of the Jews of Poland were dead. The communities where most of the survivors had once lived no longer existed. Their families and friends were all gone. In addition, anti-Semitism among the local people was widespread.

Postwar Pogroms

In 1946, about 175,000 Polish Jews who had survived the war in the Soviet Union returned to Poland. They were not welcomed home. Anti-Semitic mobs murdered hundreds of Jews between the end of the war in 1945 and the summer of 1946.

On July 4, 1946, while Americans celebrated their independence day, non-Jews in the Polish city of Kielce staged a pogrom. Before World War II, 26,000 Jews had lived in Kielce among a population of 200,000. A mere 150 returned after the war. In the Kielce pogrom, 42 Jews were killed and 50 wounded. Neither the police nor leaders of the church in the city did anything to stop the violence.

News of the Kielce pogrom spread quickly among Jews in Eastern Europe. Within three months, 100,000 Jews fled Poland and other countries in Eastern Europe. They crossed into the American- and British-controlled parts of Germany. There they joined other Jews in displaced persons' camps.

"You Are Not Abandoned."

Jewish organizations from Palestine and the United States began helping Holocaust survivors as soon as they could. They sent aid and social workers to Europe. Beginning in the fall of 1945, the U.S. Army also made efforts to improve conditions in the DP camps. By the end of the year, these efforts produced noticeable results.

In October 1945, David Ben-Gurion visited the DP camps. Ben-Gurion was the leader of the Jewish community in Palestine. However, because the British restricted immigration to Palestine, he could do little to bring the refugees there.

Ben-Gurion said to the people he met, "You are not abandoned. You are not alone. You will not live endlessly in camps like this." He promised to bring the people in the camps to Palestine "as soon as humanly possible."

Meanwhile, people in the camps slowly started to rebuild their lives on their own. Survivors got married and began having children.

Children in the camps returned to school. Many of them studied in Hebrew, the language spoken by Jews in Palestine. There were few books, blackboards, or other supplies. Often there were no trained teachers. Yet children began to learn.

Adults also attended schools. They read dozens of newspapers written by fellow survivors.

Active Learning: For your article, you may wish to take notes on how people in the DP camps began to rebuild their lives after the Holocaust.

Thinking It Over

1. How did the *Exodus* incident symbolize the strength and determination of the Holocaust survivors?
2. Why didn't Holocaust survivors want to return to Poland?

2 From Europe to Israel

Most countries remained closed to Jewish refugees after 1945. In the fall of that year, American and British delegates issued a report on conditions in the DP camps. It pointed to the poor conditions in the camps. The report also recommended that 100,000 Jews be admitted to Palestine immediately.

The British government refused to listen to the commission's recommendations. Their main concern was British access to the oil in the Middle East. This meant keeping good relations with the Arabs of the region. The Arabs opposed Jewish immigration into Palestine. Therefore,

the British did everything they could to stop Jews from entering Palestine. The Jewish refugees did everything they could to get there.

A Land of Our Own

The Jews called their effort to reach Palestine **Aliya Bet** (ah-LEE-yah bet). The word *Aliya* means "to go up to the land" in Hebrew. It refers to going up to Jerusalem, which is in the mountains. The letter *bet* is the second letter of the Hebrew alphabet. In the 1940s, Aliya Bet stood for the second way of reaching Palestine. The first way was legally. The second way was illegally.

Agents from the Jewish community of Palestine sent agents to gather Jews who had gone to Eastern and Central Europe. Their task was to gather and move refugees from these regions to Palestine

Many of the refugees were first taken to the DP camps in the American- and British-controlled parts of Germany. In the camps, they were safe and closer to their final destination.

Other refugees went to seaports in France, Italy, and Greece. From these ports, Jewish agents from Palestine helped the refugees board boats bound for Palestine.

The *Exodus* was one of those boats. Between May 1945 and May 1948, there were 64 others. All together they carried nearly 75,000 Jews to Palestine. As you may have read, most were stopped by the British and held in detention camps on the island of Cyprus. Despite the risk of being caught, many Jewish refugees were determined to go to Palestine. As one refugee explained it, "We have wandered long enough. We have worked and struggled too long on the lands of other peoples. Now we must build a land of our own."

Refugees Reach the Land of Israel

On May 14, 1948, the Jewish community of Palestine declared its independence as the State of Israel. It did so based on a decision reached

Israeli youth display the flag of the new State of Israel in July 1948, two months after Israel declared its independence. At the time of this display, Israel was in the middle of a war with the Arabs.

by the United Nations (UN) in 1947. The UN said that Palestine should be divided into two states, one Jewish and one Arab.

The Arabs refused to accept an independent Jewish state in Palestine. Armies from five Arab countries invaded Israel. Israel had to defend itself. It was now fighting for its survival as a nation.

At the same time, Israel opened its doors to all Jewish immigrants. Each month, thousands of Holocaust survivors left the camps of Europe and Cyprus and boarded boats for Israel. Between 1948 and 1950, over 270,000 Holocaust survivors entered Israel. By 1950, all of the refugees from Europe who wanted to go to Israel had arrived to begin their new lives.

The Importance of Israel

The establishment of the State of Israel is closely related to the Holocaust. Because of the Holocaust, most Jews came to believe in **Zionism.** Zionism is the idea that the Jewish people must have their own independent state in their ancient homeland in the Middle East.

The Holocaust also created support for an independent Jewish state among many non-Jews in Europe and the United States. As you have read, in September 1947 the UN voted for an independent Jewish state in part of Palestine.

There were many reasons why the creation of the State of Israel was important to the Jewish people. It gave Holocaust survivors a place to go where they would be welcomed. It also meant that in the future Jews could protect themselves from anti-Semitic violence. Jewish communities elsewhere in the world never again have to struggle alone against the hatred that resulted in the Holocaust.

Since 1948, Jews from all over the world have immigrated to Israel. In the 1940s and 1950s, 700,000 Jews fleeing persecution in Arab countries found safety in Israel. In the 1970s, and again in the 1990s, thousands of Jews left oppression in the Soviet Union and found freedom in Israel. In the 1980s and early 1990s, Israel saved over 20,000 Ethiopian Jews from war and starvation in Africa.

Jews fleeing persecution continue to go to Israel from other countries. Here they are welcomed whether they are white or black, rich or poor, religious or nonreligious. They find a home and the safety that was denied most European Jews during the Nazi era.

Thinking It Over

1. What is the connection between the Holocaust and the establishment of the State of Israel?
2. What are some of the reasons that the creation of Israel was so important to Jews around the world?

3 New Lives in the United States

When World War II ended, President Harry Truman was sympathetic toward the Jewish refugees in the DP camps. Many Americans who had read newspaper reports about the refugees' condition also wanted to help. Yet, at the same time, there was widespread anti-immigrant and anti-Semitic feeling in the United States.

As a result of these negative feelings, the United States opened its doors in 1945 only slightly to Holocaust survivors. A law passed in 1948 made it somewhat easier for Jewish refugees to enter the United States. In all, the United States admitted fewer than 100,000 Holocaust survivors in the years after World War II.

Jewish organizations helped the survivors before and after they arrived in the United States. These organizations arranged for someone to meet the refugees when they arrived in a city or town. Jewish welfare organizations also arranged to find housing and jobs for the refugees. They provided clothes, money, and guides to help newcomers find their way around. Some refugees had family members in the United States to help them. For those who did not, the Jewish welfare organizations were especially important.

In the end, the survivors had to find the strength within themselves to rebuild their lives. A large majority were able to do so. Despite their suffering and losses, they started new families and found jobs to support them.

However, many of these survivors lived their lives haunted by the past.

"We . . . Kissed Good Old American Soil."

Arriving in the United States was a great moment for many Holocaust survivors. Madeline Deutsch reached U.S. shores after being freed from Auschwitz. She was 18 years old. Madeline recalled that "practically everybody" in her group "bent down and kissed good old American soil."

However, it was not easy to get started in the United States, even for young people. Rene Fritz was almost 13 when she reached the United States. She belonged in the eighth grade, but had missed many years of school. She "had never had a day of math in my life." She spoke Yiddish and "did not understand one word" of English. To help Rene catch up, her new school came up with a plan. According to Rene:

Every day I would spend half an hour in the first grade, a half hour in the second, a half hour in the third. Well it was a little humiliating because here I am almost thirteen but there was no other way to get caught up.

Active Learning: For your article, take notes on Rene Fritz's experience in school. How would you have felt if you were in the same position?

"We Are Proud To Be Americans."

As generations of Jewish immigrants before them, Holocaust survivors grew to love the United States. Lilly Malnick came to the United States at the age of 16 after surviving Auschwitz. She said that "America gave me the chance to live as a human being again."

David Chase became a successful businessman in the United States. He stressed that "America gave us a home when we had none. . . . We are proud to be Americans."

For Holocaust survivors, coming to the United States was an important step in leaving the past behind. Yet even as they moved forward, they had to preserve the memory of the Holocaust. Many survivors began teaching younger generations about the

Holocaust. They believed that only with a knowledge and understanding of the past can we build a better future.

Holocaust Memorials and Museums

The world's most outstanding Holocaust memorial is Yad Vashem in Jerusalem, Israel. It is one of several Holocaust memorials and museums in Israel. Yad Vashem was created in 1953. In addition to a museum, it contains a research center and educational institute.

The main museum at Yad Vashem covers the period from 1933 to 1945 in photographs, films, recordings, videos, and other exhibits. Yad Vashem also has a special memorial to the 1.5 million children murdered in the Holocaust. Its "Avenue of the Righteous" honors over 10,000 non-Jews who saved Jews during the Holocaust.

The most important Holocaust memorial in the United States is the United States Memorial Museum in Washington, D.C. It opened in 1993. The museum includes a library and research materials. Another important Holocaust museum in the United States is the Museum of Tolerance at the Simon Wiesenthal Center in Los Angeles.

These museums and memorials carry the same message: The Holocaust must be remembered and its lessons must be learned.

Thinking It Over

1. How did Jewish organizations help survivors when they arrived in the United States?
2. Why do survivors teach younger generations about the Holocaust?

Forty years after the liberation of the Auschwitz-Birkenau death camp, survivors of the camp returned and marched through the camp. On their clothing, they wore the yellow Stars of David that the Nazis had made them wear during the Holocaust to identify them as Jews.

Follow-Up Review

Identifying Main Ideas

1. What was Aliya Bet?
2. Why was the establishment of Israel so important to Holocaust survivors and to the Jewish people as a whole?
3. How did Holocaust survivors react to being in the United States?

Working Together

In a small group, make a mural that captures the experiences of Jewish survivors after the Holocaust. Put the drawing on display on your bulletin board.

Active Learning

Use the notes you have taken to write a newspaper article about Holocaust survivors. Include the difficulties the survivors faced in escaping Europe and DP camps, the help they received from Jewish organizations, and their feelings and experiences when they arrived in Israel and the United States.

Lessons for Today

The Holocaust is one of the worst events in human history. Yet there are useful lessons to be learned from this tragedy. Why is it important to remember the Holocaust? What lessons are there to be learned from survivors and from history?

What Might You Have Done?

Imagine that you were a soldier in Europe at the end of World War II. You are stationed at a DP camp. Several of the survivors are arguing about whether to go to Palestine or to the United States. What would you tell them to do? Give reasons for the advice you would give them.

GLOSSARY

acquit to clear a person of criminal charges made against him or her

aggression the act of attacking a person or a group

Aktion a general raid and roundup of Jews conducted by the Nazis

Aliya Bet a Hebrew term that refers to the movement to bring Jews to Israel after the Holocaust by any means possible; literally means "to go up to the land," a reference to going up to Jerusalem, a city in the mountains of Israel

Allied Powers the nations that were fighting Germany and its allies; included Great Britain, France, the Soviet Union, and the United States

anti-Semitism acts or feelings against Jews

Arrow Cross the Hungarian version of the German Nazi party that played a huge role in deporting many of Hungary's Jews

assimilate to become more like the majority culture

Auschwitz largest concentration camp and death camp

boycott refusing to do business or associate with a certain individual or group

collaborator a person who cooperates with the enemy

concentration camp a huge prison and labor camp built by the Nazis to hold people the Nazis considered dangerous; prisoners usually died there of hard labor or starvation. There were over 100 concentration camps in Europe during the Holocaust.

crematorium a large oven or furnace where bodies of death camp inmates were burned after they had been gassed

death camp a camp built by the Nazis specifically to murder Jews; there was a total of six death camps, all located in Poland. Also called *extermination camps*.

defendant a person who is on trial for a crime

Diaspora the scattering of Jews across the world after exile from their ancient homeland

diplomat a person who represents his or her country in dealings with foreign countries

displaced person a refugee with no home to which to return

Einsatzgruppen special SS units that were assigned to kill Jews

exodus the departure of a large number of people

Final Solution the term the Nazis used to refer to their plans to completely exterminate the Jewish people

gas chamber a room that was sealed off and airtight so that death could be induced through the use of poison gas

genocide the systematic attempt to wipe out an entire people

Gestapo the secret police set up by the Nazis in 1933 to eliminate opposition to Hitler and the Nazi party; the Gestapo was known for the brutal methods it used against opponents of the Nazi regime.

ghetto a section of a city where a particular group of people is forced to live; during the Holocaust, Jews were forced to live in ghettos until they were transported by the Nazis to a concentration or extermination camp.

Holocaust the systematic, planned extermination of six million European Jews by the Nazis during World War II

Huguenot a member of a French Protestant sect

Judenrat a Jewish Council set up by the Nazis to govern the ghettos during the Holocaust

Kinderaktion a Nazi raid and roundup of pregnant women and young children

Kristallnacht an event that occurred on the night of November 9–10, 1938, when Nazis in Germany and Austria openly attacked Jewish businesses, homes, synagogues, and Jews themselves. Also known as "Crystal Night" or the "night of the broken glass," this event signaled the beginning of the Nazi effort to exterminate the Jewish people.

partisan a member of a band of civilians who operate as guerrilla fighters within enemy territory

Passover a Jewish holiday celebrating the liberation of Jews from slavery in Egypt over 3,000 years ago

pogrom a violent raid on a Jewish community

Ponary a place outside Vilna in what was then Poland and is today Lithuania, where Nazis shot and buried over 30,000 Jews during the second half of 1941

propaganda information spread to influence or mislead people

prosecute to take legal steps against someone

quota a strict limit on immigration

rabbi a Jewish religious leader

refugee a person who has been forced to flee from his or her homeland for reasons of safety

scapegoat a person that is blamed for another's problems, mistakes, or crimes

SS members of Hitler's elite force of storm troopers who were responsible for carrying out the Final Solution and running the concentration and death camps; abbreviation for *Schutzstaffel* which means "protection squads"

Star of David a six-pointed star that is a symbol of the Jewish people; during the Holocaust, Jews were forced to wear Stars of David on their clothing to identify them as Jews.

sterilize to make people unable to have children

storm trooper a member of an elite Nazi organization whose responsibilities included conducting regular attacks on Jews and anyone who challenged the Nazis

synagogue a Jewish houses of prayer and religious study

Theresienstadt a concentration camp in Czechoslovakia

tribunal a court of justice

War Refugee Board (WRB) a U.S. government agency set up by President Franklin D. Roosevelt in 1944 to help Jewish refugees and protect Jews still alive in countries allied to Germany

Yiddish a language developed by European Jews between the 800s and the 1100s, it blends German, Hebrew, and the languages of Eastern Europe

Zionism a movement to create and maintain an independent Jewish state in the ancient homeland of the Jews in the Middle East

Zyklon B a poison gas the Nazis used to kill victims in gas chambers

INDEX

A

Acquittal, *103*
Aggression, *102*
Aktions, *69*
Aliya Bet, *117*
Allied Powers, *94*
Anielewicz, Mordechai, *38, 45, 46*
Anti-Semitism, *10, 22, 53, 79, 91*
    in Christian teachings, *15-16*
    of Crusaders, *6, 16-17*
    in Germany, *17, 20*
    of Hitler, *9, 24, 25-26, 35*
    in Poland, *17, 18*
    scapegoating and, *26-27*
Arrow Cross, *84*
Aryan race, *9, 25, 53*
Assimilation, *17*
Auschwitz, *10, 52, 55, 56, 84*
    bombing raids on, *95-96, 97*
    death camp at, *57-61, 96, 106*
    liberation of, *96*
Austria
    Nazi invasion of, *9, 91*
    in World War *I, 25*
Austrian Jews, *105*

B

Babi Yar massacre, *53*
Baeck, Leo, *30*
Bass, Franta, *66*
Belzec, *55*
Ben-Gurion, David, *105, 116*
Bergen-Belsen, *98*
Berg, Mary, *69*
Berlin, Germany, *28, 29, 33*
Bialer, Tosha, *41*
Birkenau, *55, 58*
Black Death, *16*
Book-burning, *28*
Boycott of Jewish businesses, *28, 29*
Britain, refugee policy of, *91, 92, 114-15, 117, 118*
Buchenwald, *82*

C

Cannon, James, Jr., *93*
Chase, David, *119*
Chelmno, *55, 106*
Children
    in concentration camps, *66, 67*
    in displaced person camps, *116-17*
    German Jews, *29*
    in ghettos, *41-42, 69-73*
    in hiding, *69, 71, 72, 73-74, 78, 81, 82*
    killing of, *66, 68, 116*
    roundup of, *69, 79-80*
Christianity, anti-Semitic teachings in, *15- 16*
Collaborators, *79*
Concentration camps, *7, 9-10, 20, 27, 28, 32, 58*
    children in, *66, 67*
    location of, *54*
    See also Death camps
Crematoria, *59, 61, 96*
Crusaders, *6, 16-17*
Czechoslovakia, Nazi invasion of, *9*
Czerniakow, Adam, *43, 45*

D

Dachau, *27, 28, 32*
Danish Jews, *83*
Datner, Szymon, *55*
Death camps, *6, 7, 31, 52*
    Auschwitz, *57-61, 96, 106*
    classification of Jews for, *53-54*
    Eichmann and, *105-6*
    liberation of, *96, 98*
    location of, *54, 55*
    transport to, *52, 53, 55-56, 57*
Defendents, *103, 104, 109*
DeNazification, *104*
Deutsch, Madeline, *119*
Diaspora, *12-13*
Dinur, Yehiel, *109*
Diplomat, *84*

Displaced person (DP) camps, *115, 116-18*
Douwes, Arnold, *82*
Duckwitz, Georg D., *83*

E

Economic depression, in Germany, *8-9, 26*
Edelman, Marek, *46*
Eichmann, Adolf, *53, 66*
    capture of, *102, 106-7*
    role in Holocaust, *105-6*
    trial of, *107-9*
Einsatzgruppen, *38-39, 52, 53, 68, 103, 116*
Einstein, Albert, *20*
Evian Conference, *91-92*
Exodus, 114
Exodus incident, *114-15, 118*

F

Fajks, Eduard, *80*
Final Solution, *41, 53, 63-64*
Frank, Anne, *73*
Frankl, Victor, *59*
French Jews, *79-80, 82*
Fritz, Rene, *119*

G

Gas chambers, *59, 60, 61*
Genocides, *6*
German Jews, *5-6, 7*
    and anti-Semitism, *17, 20*
    baiting of, *30*
    community life of, *17, 18*
    emigration of, *20, 31, 32, 90, 91, 92*
    and Kristallnacht, *24, 31-33, 92*
    Nazi persecution of, *28-30, 36*
Germany
    division of, *104*
    economic depression in, *8-9, 26*
    in World War *I, 8, 20, 25, 26*
    See also Hitler, Adolf; Nazi regime

ACKNOWLEDGMENTS

Grateful acknowledgment is made to the following publishers, authors, and other copyright holders:

p. 19: From *A Jewish Boyhood in Poland: Remembering Kolbuszowa*, by Norman Salsitz. NY: Syracuse University Press, 1992, pp. 73-76. Used by permission of Syracuse University Press. *p. 22:* From *History of the Holocaust*, by Yehuda Bauer. NY: Franklin Watts Inc., 1982, pp. 8-9. Used by permission of Franklin Watts Inc. *p. 33: From When Time Ran Out: Coming of Age in the Third Reich*, by Frederick Zeller. NY: The Permanent Press, 1989, pp. 138-139. Used by permission of The Permanent Press. *p. 49:* From *The Jews of Warsaw: 1939-1943 Ghetto, Underground, Revolt*, by Yisrael Guttman. IN: Indiana University Press, 1982, pp. 397, 429-430. Used by permission of Indiana University Press. *p. 60:* From *Auschwitz Seen by the SS*, by Johann Paul Kremer. Poland: Oswiecim, 1978, pp. 438-439. Globe Fearon Educational Publisher has executed a reasonable and concerted effort to contact the publisher of *Auschwitz Seen by the SS*. We eagerly invite any persons knowledgeable about the publisher to contact Globe Fearon Educational Publisher to arrange for the customary publishing transactions. *pp. 63-64:* From *The Nazi Holocaust*, by Ronnie S. Landau, copy right © 1992, 1994 by Ronnie S. Landau. By permission of Ivan R. Dee Inc. *pp. 66-67:* From *... I never saw another butterfly... Children's Drawings and Poems fron Terezín Concentration Camp*, ed. Hana Volavkova. NY: Schocken Books, 1993, pp. 39 and 55. Used by permission of Schocken Books. *p. 81:* Reprinted from *The Last Selection: A Child's Journey through the Holocaust*, by Goldie Szachter Kalib with Sylan Kalib and Ken Wachsberger (Amherst: The University of Massachusetts Press, 1991), Copyright © 1991 by Goldie Kalib, Sylvan Kalib, and Ken Wachsberger. *p. 97:* From *The World Must Know*, by Michael Berembaum (quotation of Elie Wiesel). Boston: Little Brown and Company, 1993, pp. 145. Used by permission of the U.S. Holocaust Memorial Museum. *p. 108:* From *Justice in Jerusalem*, by Gideon Hausner. New York: Harper and Row, 1966, pp. 388-390. Globe Fearon Educational Publisher has executed a reasonable and concerted effort to contact the author of the speech by Gideon Hausner. We eagerly invite any persons knowledgeable about the whereabouts of the authors or agents to contact Globe Fearon Educational Publisher to arrange for the customary publishing transactions.

Grateful acknowledgment is made to the following for illustrations, photographs, and reproductions on the pages indicated.

Photo credits: Cover: The Bettmann Archive; *Title Page:* The Bettmann Archive; *p. 5:* The Bettmann Archive; *p. 7:* Main Commission for the Investigation of Nazi War Crimes, courtesy of the United States Holocaust Memorial Museum; *p. 8:* UPI/Bettmann; *p. 9:* The National Archives; *p. 10:* UPI/Bettmann Newsphotos; *p. 11:* The Bettmann Archive; *p. 12:* The Bettmann Archive; *p. 14:* The Granger Collection; *p. 16:* The Bettmann Archive; *p. 23:* The National Archives; *p. 26:* Courtesy of the United States Holocaust Memorial Museum; *p. 27:* The Bettmann Archive; *p. 28:* The National Archives, courtesy of the United States Holocaust Memorial Museum; *p. 29:* Yad Vahsem, courtesy of the United States Holocaust Memorial Museum; *p. 31:* Library of Congress; *p. 32:* Rijsinstituut voor Oorlogdocumentatie, courtesy of the United States Holocaust Memorial Museum; *p. 37:* Main Commission for the Investigation of Nazi War Crimes, courtesy of the United States Holocaust Memorial Museum; *p. 39:* The Bettmann Archive; *p. 40:* Jewish Historical Institute, courtesy of the United States Holocaust Memorial Museum; *p. 44:* Yad Vahsem, courtesy of the United States Holocaust Memorial Museum; *p. 46:* Bildarchiv Preussischer Kulturbesitz, courtesy of the United States Holocaust Memorial Museum; *p. 47:* The Bettmann Archive; *p. 51:* The National Archives, Suitland, MD, courtesy of the United States Holocaust Memorial Museum; *p. 52:* Library of Congress, courtesy of the United States Holocaust Memorial Museum; *p. 56:* Yad Vashem, courtesy of the United States Holocaust Memorial Museum; *p. 58:* Yad Vashem, courtesy of the United States Holocaust Memorial Museum; *p. 65:* The National Archives, courtesy of the United States Holocaust Memorial Museum; *p. 65:* Yad Vashem, courtesy of the United States Holocaust Memorial Museum; *p. 68:* Main Commission for the Investigation of Nazi War Crimes, courtesy of the United States Holocaust Memorial Museum; *p. 70:* Jerzy Tomaszewski, courtesy of the United States Holocaust Memorial Museum; *p. 71:* The Bettmann Archive; *p. 72:* Courtesy of the United States Holocaust Memorial Museum; *p. 73:* The Bettmann Archive; *p. 77:* Museum of Denmark's Fight for Freedom, courtesy of the United States Holocaust Memorial Museum; *p. 78:* UPI/Bettmann; *p. 79:* Nancy Seisel/NYT Photo; *p. 82:* Peter Feigl, courtesy of the United States Holocaust Memorial Museum; *p. 84:* Thomas Veres, courtesy of the United States Holocaust Memorial Museum; *p. 85:* Courtesy of the United States Holocaust Memorial Museum; *p. 89:* UPI/Corbis-Bettmann; *p. 95:* The National Archives, courtesy of the United States Holocaust Memorial Museum; *p. 96:* The National Archives; *p. 97:* The National Archives, courtesy of the United States Holocaust Memorial Museum; *p. 98:* The National Archives; *p. 101:* UPI/Bettmann Newsphotos; *p. 103:* The National Archives; *p. 105:* The Bettmann Archives; *p. 107:* UPI/Bettmann; *p. 113:* UPI/Bettmann Newsphotos; *p. 114:* Central Zionist Archives, courtesy of the United States Holocaust Memorial Museum; *p. 117:* UPI/Bettmann; *p. 120:* Reuters/Bettmann.